BURNT CHAPEL

_____
_____

a novella by

CODY EICHELBERGER

Best wishes!

CODY EICHELBERGER'S

BURNT CHAPEL

FOR KAREN

CODY EICHELBERGER'S

BURNT CHAPEL

ACKNOWLEDGEMENTS

The following individuals have made this experience possible:

Jessica Prosser

Nancy Funk

Stephanie A. Jirard

Diana Sheffield

and my wife, Brittany Eichelberger

BURNT CHAPEL

1

Rule #1: never cross the boundary.

Paul made the rule perfectly sound before she drifted off from their remote cabin in the woods to where the stream came together at a sharp angle. It was forbidden to cross the stream, and she knew Paul had his ways of finding out whether or not she was actually doing it. She approached the sand bank with a plastic bucket in her right hand and her feet in the water. Minnows gathered there for their morning feeding. The sun had not risen yet, but it was clear enough to see the mist whirl three feet above the gray.

I wish Bethany was here to see this, she thought.

She reached down and touched the surface of the water with her fingertips. Cold waves radiated up her forearm and sent shivers down to her toes. What she wanted was to get a little closer so she could take a sip. Nothing felt more enriching than to feel chilled water roll down a dry esophagus--a brief gift that only lasts three seconds. But rules were rules and must be followed. A cold drink would have to wait.

Ava reached for the plastic bucket she carried with her and stuck half of it into the water. She listened to the bottom fill up rapidly. When the steel handle began to bend at the middle, she pulled it up with intense strength. Making sure the bucket was free from debris, she rushed towards the bank with the heavy weight bucket by her side. Time was of the essence.

You got this Ava, she thought. *You may not make it out of the woods in one piece but with some elbow grease you can work wonders.*

Ava forgot how peaceful it was in the woods. Woodpeckers worked like lumberjacks, hammering their beaks into the wood. The sound traveled far and beyond like somebody knocking on something thin and hollow. She rested by a lonesome hemlock, wiping beads of sweat from her brow. Other than the hard working pecker somewhere South of Ava, the woods remained silent. From time-to-time, the heads of the pines would sway which would make this creepy creaking sound. She looked up to the pines and the sky. The sun started to rise. Time to get moving.

Her feet carried her down a dirt trail, weakened by so many trips to the stream. No longer than a mile, the trail was crafted by Paul himself. Without the use of machinery, the trail demanded time consumption and dedication. A month of solid work did the trick thanks to a shovel, some rain, and a shallow coating of shale. Over time, the trail molded itself into a God given masterpiece.

Ava batted the mosquitoes from her face. Dozens buzzed nearby like little devils with wings. Thirsty for fresh blood, they ignored Ava's feelings of them and began to torment.

Darn things, she whispered.

Girls were taught at an early age to wear dresses and sometimes skirts given the occasion. Permission granted by the husband, the first wife was often permitted the luxury to wear skirts while other wives shared by the same husband wore nothing else than a blue or white dress. Ava wore a robin egg skirt, and when she looked down at the trim, she spotted something that often haunted her nightmares.

A rush of anxiety swept through her body like a ghost as she settled the bucket of water on the carpet of pine needles. With her heart pulsing and forehead wet with perspiration, she pinched the trim of her dress and rubbed it raw. The water from all of the brisk walking had leaped from inside the bucket

3

and landed on the trim. Anyone who knew Paul knows that he had a temper of a jackal. If he would have seen the wet spot on that dress--

Ava worked her fingers into the fabric until the wet spot faded completely. Sure, there was an imprint in the fabric from all the rubbing but sure enough, the spot was gone. She took a breather before reaching for the bucket again, making sure not to spill anymore. That was the good news.

The bad news?

Too much time was wasted on listening to singing birds and wet spots. Things were to escalate quickly if Paul wasn't on another one of his hunting trips. She imagined him at the cabin raising a ruckus over a bucket of water and since it wouldn't be delivered on time, Ava would get the shaft. With no time to waste, she walked a steady pace.

She thought about Bethany and what she was up to at the cabin. If Paul didn't leave the cabin, Ava imagined he would put the woman to work. God knows there was plenty of it especially when Paul would be out hunting with his bow for hours on end, leaving them stuck in the cabin for hours throughout the day with no one to talk to.

Six years sounds like pennies and dimes to a city dweller but deep in the Pennsylvania woods, it feels like a lifetime. Those six years were spent on obeying Paul's strict rules of marriage for his satisfaction, not hers. Every day wasn't a total loss. Ava learned throughout the years that Paul craved sexual pleasure with his women. If he was happy beneath the covers, he was happy everywhere else. But sometimes that happiness dies down and they're left to clean up the mess.

Ava and Bethany called Paul's temper swings flares. Every time he'd get mad, he was on a flare. She could only remember one time when the flare was so bad, he had broken Bethany's left arm with a skillet because she had cooked his eggs for too long. Luckily, Ava knew how to treat the broken bone by making a sling out of a shirt but the lasting effect from the broken arm caused Bethany to have aches and pains every now and then. Sometimes when Bethany would extend her arm the wrong way, the whole arm would go numb followed by a pins-and-needles sensation.

The trail rose above a mossy bank where an opening in the trees led Ava to a small clearing. Five yards from the opening stood a wooden chapel and its three stained glass windows. The forest-green shingled roof came up at an angle where a steel Cross handcrafted by Paul himself shot into the cloudy sky. A rose garden surrounded the chapel on three sides.

Aside from the rose garden, the chapel remained hidden due to the overgrowth of vegetation. Three bushes climbed along the left side of the religious structure, rising above the Cross. Grapes grew there as well as a raspberry tree.

Paul's cabin stood nearby to the chapel, perhaps an additional five yards behind it. The cabin was a two-story building constructed of pine. The logs were dark and preserved with chemicals to prevent insects from eating their way through. Porcupines used to be a problem as they'd gradually chew their way through the wood. Paul fixed the problem by pumping them full of buck shot. It's been three years since they'd seen a porcupine.

The cabin stood on a small hill which overlooked the valley for several miles. As for many cabins in the area, this one was not in bad shape. Having six windows on the second floor stretching across the front panel, two windows on the first floor, and a screened-in porch, it looked like a residential paradise.

Two hemlocks towered over the shingled roof from both sides, creeping their bony limbs across the porch. At night when the moon is bright, these limbs can be seen from the front yard. One could easily mistake them for skeleton arms. Their roots had grown beneath the porch, causing the boards to uplift from their once-stationary state. Nothing could be done about the boards except for removing the hemlocks completely. The damage from the shift also affected the porch beams.

Ava took the bucket of water towards the right side of the porch where she was greeted with a screen door. She opened it, releasing a sigh of relief, and walked in. The porch appeared dark from the overcast outside. The boards were hidden beneath a green carpet and three rocking chairs. Two of the chairs were rocking on their own at the other end of the porch while the other rocked a steady pace in the dark corner to Ava's right. A figure occupied the chair. It's shadow danced off of the cabin's side next beside a wooden sign with green lettering that read: Lot. 4-06.

Ava stood by the door with the bucket by her side. She stared at the shadow while her heart raced nearly out of its cage. Her eyes began at the thick black boots which met the trim of blue denim. The light disappeared by the knees at which the darkness quickly took over. The figure wore a flannel shirt tucked inside a black belt. His arms were too long for the rocking chairs, causing his veiny hands to dangle off the wood. His long hair came to the base of his shoulders, gray and ugly looking. Age did not do any favors for this man. As for his face, it remained a mystery behind the curtain of darkness

He rocked there in silence for a few moments before he spoke for the first time. His voice was deep and raspy as if he had just gotten done with a nasty coughing spell. Ava trembled.

"You're late," the raspy voice said. The face remained hidden from her. Goosebumps covered her arms.

"I'm sorry Paul," she replied.

Please god, don't let him see the wet spot, she prayed.

"How long have you been living here Ava?"

Her eyes dropped to the bucket of water. It was still. Not a single ripple.

"Six years."

"*Six years*," he replied, nodding as if to confirm her answer.

The rocking chair abruptly blasted the side of the cabin, rattling the Lot. 4-06 sign on its rusty nail. The man rose from the darkness and into the light, crossing the porch towards the wooden railing. His sea blue eyes captured the valley below them. Ava spied on the bucket again, making sure there wasn't a drop missing before her eyes settled on the blue checkered flannel he was wearing. *Whoa! We have a color everybody!*

His rough hands, like bear claws, dug into the wood.

"In those six long years with me, what have you learned?"

"Not to waste time."

He nodded while scratching his beard which was more of a light brown than gray. He turned his head towards Ava, keeping his body still. A devilish grin stretched across his face, causing his sharp cheekbones to rise.

"You've wasted it plenty, haven't you?"

"It won't happen again," she said, reaching for the bucket.

Instantly, Paul's presence was close when she found him within inches away from her face. Every hair on his face was accounted for as he breathed into her eyes.

"Remember the rules," he said. "Deviate just one, I'll bury you six feet underground. God knows I will. Understand?"

"I understand."

She picked the bucket of water up from the porch and walked into the cabin. She didn't say another word.

2

It was late in the afternoon.

Ava took one of the buckets and poured the water into the sink basin. Their lifestyle in Lot. 4-06 was primitive and very basic. Running water did not exist there. Face and hand washing took place at the sink basin. Baths were upstairs.

The downstairs consisted of an open room. Three beams separated the room into three different sections. The kitchen area and living room were to the right of the cabin whereas an empty space with three book shelves was to the left by the staircase.

The walls were all made of pine just as the outside. Everything looked so brown that even Ava felt like she was wooden at times. She stood by the sink with her wet hands in the basin. Sick in the stomach, she cupped her hands together and brought her face forward. Bethany came up from behind and wrapped her arms around Ava's abdomen.

"You are scaring me," Bethany said.

Ava jumped of fright as beads of water rolled down her cheeks. She dried them and faced Bethany who was red in the face. She wore a gray dress and a white bonnet. Ava always thought Bethany was the prettiest one. She imagined that is why Paul married Bethany but there was more to the story. Bethany learned how to cook at a very young age, and she was a wicked wizard at gardening.

"How so?"

Bethany wrapped her fingers around Ava's thin pelvis.

"You're nothing but skin and bones. If you keep doing this Ava there will be nothing left of you. Are you eating anything?"

"Just dinner."

"Ava!"

"Just stop it. Please."

Bethany pressed her lips together while tightening the straps to her bonnet.

"I just don't get it. Why do you do it then?" Bethany asked. "Is it for yourself or for him?"

Ava paused before providing an answer to the difficult question.

"It makes me feel better."

Bethany did not look convinced.

"Well, whatever   it is you have, it's going to kill you someday Ava. Best keep an eye on it before your slim eating habits go too far. I wouldn't like to see you end up in the grave before your twenty-fifth birthday."

A moment of silence crept between them at the table. The fireplace was to the left of Ava, an empty vessel that hasn't breathed an ember in weeks. The season of summer was coming to a gradual end.

A plate of turkey sandwiches sat in the center while broccoli, cauliflower, and tomatoes surrounded it. Bethany looked up from her empty plate and grinned. Ava frowned. Eating felt like a chore to her, something she was better off not bothering with.

Paul joined them at the table. He held out his hands to them. They accepted.

"Ava," he said. "Would you lead us in prayer?"

Oh no, she thought. *So unpredictable. What should I pray about? If there is anything in this world I hate is being put on the spot to such an embarrassing ritual. How cruel of this man to make me do this. So cruel.*

"Ava!" he shouted. Saliva squirted the shiny table before him as he settled his sapphire jewels on her blushed cheeks. "Maybe Beth ought to sit you down and teach you the hours of time considering you must have forgotten it. What is it with you today? Get on with it before I get irritated."

In sudden panic, Ava closed her eyes and thought of anything she could to make this man happy.

"Bless this food Lord," she prayed. "Give us strength as we continue each day in your grace. Keep Paul safe when he hunts. Watch over Bethany throughout her day and keep our garden fruitful."

Thank God it's over, Ava thought, weeping on the inside.

3

When they finished lunch, Paul went upstairs to dress up in his hunting gear while Bethany and Ava washed the dishes. Washing dishes became a norm in their daily life while Paul would hike half the day hunting game. But there was more than washing dishes at the cabin. There were other chores that must be completed before Paul's return. These chores consisted of dusting all the wood because dust chews through wood over time. Paul never liked dust, and he had an eye for it. Sometimes, when they weren't paying attention, he'd swipe his finger across the rails or along the walls for any sign. He'd look beneath the couches, the beds, and the dressers for dust bunnies. And God help them if he'd find any sign of them.

Paul came down the steps and turned left to where the girls were standing. He wore a camouflage shirt tucked into his blue denim. Ava knew clothes like that existed on the outside of their little world. They were required to sew their own. He fixed his sleeves before approaching the closet door. He opened it and fetched his bow. The apparatus was an intimidating piece of hunting machinery that could hold several arrows along the side and even featured a ruby eye piece for accuracy. He held it in the light like He-Man pointing his magnificent sword to the sky.

"You will finish your chores while I am gone."

He slipped his arm through the bow and opened the front door. A September breeze chilled them both. But before he left, he approached his two wives, kissed them on the cheek, and threw on a baseball cap with the Phillies logo stitched in white thread. He headed out, closing the door behind him.

4

Ava had Johnny Cash on the record player downstairs while they worked on dusting the furnishings. Ava hummed along to *I Still Miss Someone* as she climbed on her hands and knees to gather the disgusting dust bunnies floating beneath the couch. She used a dusty old rag stained with oil polish.

Bethany worked on the shelves and the fireplace mantel, removing every picture frame and decorative piece to get to the dust. She did not approve of Ava's willingness to put on Paul's music. The girls were forbidden to enter his record room but Ava seemed to breathe her own air when Paul was gone.

Later that afternoon, once all the dusting was finished, Ava took Bethany's hand and they ran off into the woods. Such a practice in Paul's presence would have been dismissed very quickly if he was there, but he wasn't. He wouldn't be home for a couple hours.

Instead of taking their usual walk down the ordinary trail, Ava steered Bethany into the deep woods. Ava had burst into irresistible laughter as she ran. Bethany tried to keep up, leaping over fallen birch trees and avoiding the thorn bushes.

The air was cooler under the shade. They passed the mossy mounds where toads were plumped down on their warty lard, blinking their eyes casually, just waiting for a fly to come buzzing by their hot zone. They passed the pines swaying in the breeze. They sounded like growling monsters as the wind rattled their pointy tops against one another, swishing like ocean waves along the shore.

"Where are we going silly?" Bethany said, laughing. Still, she felt afraid.

What if we get lost out here? she thought.

But no matter how scared Ava made Bethany, there was no going back. Ava wanted more. In fact, she *craved* for more.

Ava chuckled as she jumped over another mossy mound. Mushrooms of all types had found a rut to grow in. Bethany took a quick glance at them growing along the fallen birch and wondered if Paul would be mad if she brought back a skirt full back with her. She'd fry them on the stove and serve it as a side dish for supper. But then, she knew what question would follow as he'd lick his fingers clean: *where did you find these delicious caps*?

"Ava," Bethany said, still laughing. She reached for Ava's dress and missed. "Where are you taking me?"

"Just wait and see," Ava hollered back. "You will love it."

"But the trails," Bethany said. "You'll get us lost."

"You're such a worry wart," Ava said. "I've done this many times before."

The sound of that made Bethany queasy. What about Paul? What will he say when he finds out about this? Or worst yet, what would become of them if Ava got too carried away and didn't know her way back? They would be stranded, deep in the woods, with nothing but the clothes on their backs. Bethany was a firm believer in the fact that over the last four years, she became a house cat. Unaware of the wild, she was sure to die if Ava wasn't careful.

"Ava," she said. "I think it's time to go—"

"We are here," Ava said. She came to a stop.

A cluster of pines shaded them from the burning sun in the sky. Bethany smelled the potent aroma of skunk and creek water. Where this vermin was hiding, she couldn't tell. But the skunk was nearby.

Locusts chanted in the distance, making their rattles the king noise of the forest.

"Ava," Bethany said. "It's beautiful out here, but I think we should get back to the cabin before Paul returns. You know how he gets."

"Beth," Ava said, grabbing Bethany by her shoulders. "I want you to listen to me."

Oh no, Bethany thought. *She's thinking about escaping. No way. There is no way I'm standing behind her on this. We are going back to the cabin and waiting for Paul to come back. We will make dinner together like we always do and we will—*

"I want you to forget about Paul for a moment," she said. "There is something very special I've been wanting to show you. Can you promise me you will at least try this?"

"Depends," Bethany said.

"Promise me," Ava said, holding out her pinky. "Please."

Bethany accepted the request and followed Ava into the thicket. Thorns snagged at her dress, ripping three slashes across her legs. Ava took Bethany's hand and led her further into the bushes where the forest opened up into a wide clearing. A powerful stream started in the distance beneath an old train track bridge. Vines grew to incredible lengths, completely covering the entire bridge.

The stream began on a shelf and suddenly dropped to the second level where they stood. Mist exploded from the drop off and hovered over the cold water for a few yards before it evaporated.

"It's the most beautiful thing I have ever seen," Bethany said. "How did you find this place?"

Ava approached the sandy bank where she had collected her water. The chill made her quiver.

"Six years ago when I met Paul," she said. She slipped her shoe off, removed the white stocking, and dipped her white foot into the water. She closed her eyes as her mind traveled a journey of a thousand seas. Things were different here, much different. Everything melted away. All the worries in the world no longer mattered. The chill sent a radiating sensation to her pelvis where the sensation released a shock wave to the inner center of her belly. "I wandered off the perimeter and found this place while he was hunting. I've been coming here ever since. This is where I come to erase what I've done in my life. All of the bad and the evil just goes away."

Ava turned towards Bethany. Her feet were still in the water.

"Do you remember your previous life?" Ava asked.

Bethany met Ava by the bank and sat by the cemetery of freshwater clam shells. She picked one up and fingered the rough plate of swirling purples and blues.

"You mean the life I had before I met Paul?"

"Of course."

"Wasn't much of a life," Bethany said, giving the shell a toss into the stream. "What I had before Paul was a pretty dim history. You know this."

"You rarely discuss this topic."

"Because this topic is not worth bringing up."

Ava sat on the sand and crossed her arms on her knees.

"You love him, don't you?" Ava asked. "You've always loved him."

"You don't?"

Ava chuckled, a sign that brought Bethany to understand the complexity of the question.

Bring on the soap box, Bethany thought. *I think I just opened a can of worms.*

"The decision wasn't mine to decide."

"You're afraid," Bethany said. Her eyes were on Ava's white bonnet which decided to come off after sitting in the sticky humidity. A lock of crimson hair dropped to the dip in her shoulder followed by an avalanche of red hair. She folded the bonnet and placed it in the grass. "You're afraid of loving him."

"You have no idea what his motive is," Ava said. "He's bleeding us dry. For years we've been following the same rules we've been taught. And what is the meaning behind these rules? I'll tell you what they mean. They mean control. If the rules didn't exist there wouldn't be a marriage. You rob the zebra his stripes, he's no longer a zebra. His performance out there in the real world, wherever that may be, would ruin him. We are slaves Bethany. Shackled ball-and-chain, you and I are making him see things that aren't there."

"We shouldn't be talking about him behind his back," Bethany said.

Ava burst into laughter.

"Or what?" Ava said, on the verge of tears. "He'll come leaping out from the woods in a reign of terror? Wake up Beth. You're a sleeper. He's been sipping your brains out with a straw ever since he married you. It's all one giant conspiracy. Can I ask you a question? A serious question?"

"Please do," Bethany said. *Anything to make you happy Ava.*

"If Paul would die tomorrow, could you survive on your own? Could you support yourself after being battered all these years?"

"He wouldn't do that to us."

Tears streamed down Ava's cheeks.

"You're far too gone, aren't you?" Ava asked, wiping her cheeks clean with her palm. She swallowed the dry lump in her throat when she stood up. She looked at Bethany with swollen eyes and gently began to remove her dress. The white dress dropped to Ava's ankles exposing her petite breasts and freckled shoulders. Bethany already felt envious as she spied on Ava's pink nipples. Then, there was the red patch. *Ohhh*, how beautiful she was. "If you want to be his sheep and follow orders, then that is your God given right."

Ava turned away from Bethany and stared at the small island of sand in the center of the stream. A tree stump stood at an angle on the island where Ava had stored her collection of clam shells.

"Afraid to love, you say?" Ava whispered, grinning. "You can't love what you never had to begin with. I am not a sheep. I am a person and I say to hell with the rules."

5

Oh, no! Please, no!

The dark woods unfastened like a metal sardine can being flayed open. The pine trees curled their tops and met their roots as the sky bled red beyond the distant horizon. The landscape didn't waste any time by twisting itself into a kaleidoscope especially when the trees seemed nonexistent after clashing against one another. It sounded like bones being crushed under pressure. From behind a stump, Ava watched as the horror unraveled.

This is a dream. It has to be. It will lead its course for the night and hopefully disappear. I'll wake up and everything will be fine.

But everything was far from fine.

The mountain cracked its back when it started to curl in unison with the pines. Birds flocked by the hundreds to the red sky, horrified by the destruction of their environment. She watched these birds darken the earth beneath them like a reaper shadow that would keep her in the dark forever. They chirped together making the noise unbearable to the comfort of the human ear.

The land beyond the cliff rose like a century year old python waking up from a long hibernation. Dust stormed over its scaly belly of trees and mountains, rising higher and higher. Shaken by the buttery meltdown overtaken by the tormented sky, Ava started to run. She ran as fast as she could through the untouched woodland, unaware of what she might find along the journey. The sky followed her, burning the presence of scarlet in the darkness. The potent odor of brimstone sucked the air dry. Robbed of fresh air, Ava suffered tremendously. Feeling as though her lungs collapsed, she dropped to her knees, and clutched her throat. Every gasp of air ended in a coughing spell.

It's finally happening now. I'm going to die. It will be slow, and it will be excruciatingly painful.

The rising mountain couldn't hold up much longer and crashed down on itself. Ava felt the earth rattle from down under. The eruption of dust and debris would approach at a phenomenal speed and swallow her whole. But running away wasn't so easy this time. She coughed and wheezed as her chest tightened.

Prepared to be hammered by the harrowing blast, she stole her last breath. That's when she saw it. A chapel stood amongst the trees with a silver moonlit outline around its border. She had seen this place before. Not in real time but in her nightmares. The chapel itself was coal-black in color trapped between a nest of vines. A hellish fire burned within its confines and bled out the stained glass windows. The flames danced on the ferns like a Kokopelli. The chapel door gave off a ruby illumination, practically indicating its haunting presence.

The chapel not only portrayed a glowing red door but it began to grow. The silver moonlit border broke away, allowing the chapel to crawl out from its grave and into the clearing. Limbs with claws on them dug into the needle carpet from all corners. It came alive.

Dust particles hovered above her head. The blast behind her was close. She tried lifting her legs but it did her no good. Ava was stuck and helpless. In a matter of seconds, her body would be seared beyond repair. She dug her nails between her breasts and closed her eyes. The ground trembled and snarled. The heat kissed her back like hundreds of little fire ants.

It's here.

Before the atomic wave could reach her, she saw the chapel speeding towards her.

That's when she woke up in a pool of sweat, safe and sound under the covers.

6

The third Sunday of every month was sacred.

The following morning came a day to recognize their symbolic marriage. Attendance was required as well as proper clothing. Paul spent the morning in the bath tub while Steelhart's *I'll Never Let You Go* lifted from the record player outside the cracked door. Outside the door on the handle hung a black suit and dress shoes.

When his bath session concluded, Paul stepped out onto a towel and dried his naked body. Dispatching the wet towel to the corner, he reached for one of his blades and started to shave.

Slowly, he thought.

The blade followed the trail of white cream before it ducked under the sink water for a swift rinse. He brought it back up again. Little grains of hair dirtied the sink water as he'd dip the blade in each time. When he was finished, he rinsed the blade off and laid it aside. He padded his cheeks and chin before pausing at the mirror. Miniature bumps of irritated skin rallied into clusters along his cheeks and neck. The skin felt sticky at the touch and boy, didn't it burn.

The record slept peacefully in the hallway after it struck its last bead. Paul removed the record, returned the disc into its sleeve, and walked it to the last room down the hall. It was a room full of records performed by hundreds of artists. He had them organized by genre and on their individual shelving units. He walked into the genre of rock and returned the sleeve to its rightful place.

He stood at the door and was ready to close it. That's when he noticed his Johnny Cash record out of place.

7

"Do you believe in premonitions?"

Bethany thought about the question while she tried on her white dress. She really had no idea what a premonition was in the first place. But she gave it a shot anyway, hoping it would be enough for Ava to move on.

"I'm not sure. Why do you ask?"

Ava tore the knotted strands of hair from the teeth in the brush and gave it a toss into the waste basket. She sent the brush through her red hair again with much ease.

"I had a dream last night," Ava said. Too emotional to keep the brush going, she stopped and looked into the mirror. "A nightmare, actually. I was somewhere in the woods and the ground just lifted."

"That's odd," Bethany replied, trying on her stockings.

"It was dreadful yet it felt so real."

"I've had dreams like that Ava." Bethany walked across the room and closed the door. She undid her dress and reached for another. Unsatisfied by the second choice, she proceeded with the first. "Don't get stirred up by dreams and illusions. Paul says--"

"Oh, forget about what Paul says!" Ava shouted. She continued to brush. "He thinks he has all the answers but he doesn't. He's fooling you and he's fooling me."

Ava slammed the brush down on the dresser.

"He isn't even religious."

"Don't say that Ava!"

Bethany met Ava at the dresser with her fists clutched. Ava saw them but she didn't care anymore. If Bethany would happen to deliver a swing, she'd be ready to pop one back.

"I saw the chapel last night," Ava said. Her eyes met Bethany's in the mirror. She looked at the blonde curls on Bethany's small head and wondered how many times she tried brushing without having to stop and tear out the knots. "If my dreams are even remotely true, then we have another thing coming."

"You're wrong," Bethany said. Her temper surfaced. "Maybe if you follow the rules every now and then, you'd probably see differently."

"The rules," Ava joked. "You're still lost, aren't you? You still believe he loves you. You're just as much as a fool as he is. It's a whirlwind full of stupidity."

"Take it back Ava."

Bethany's fists tightened.

"I see whose side your on."

Bethany had about five seconds to knock whatever foolishness was clogging Ava's brain but when she counted to three, she was two seconds too late. The bedroom door swung open and Paul stepped in. Bethany spun around and loosened her grip while Ava made the final touches to her hair.

"I heard fighting in here," he said. His face was cleanly shaven except for the razor burn. He came to them and stood stern with his eyes on Ava. "I'm not a experienced psychic but I'm sure you've ruffled Bethany's feathers up somehow. Am I right-t?"

Ava shuddered at Paul's emphasis on the *t* and didn't mind the brush anymore. She directed her full attention to Paul.

"Bethany and I were just talking. Weren't we?"

Ava looked at Bethany.

Paul did the same.

"It's true Paul," she said. "Ava and I were only talking."

"It's time then," he said. "Meet me downstairs in five minutes. Don't keep me waiting."

8

A stone path guided them from the porch steps to the chapel. They walked towards the chapel side-by-side with Paul in the middle. He held their hands delicately while Ava felt the fear blossom into a cancerous growth inside her stomach. They were walking towards a representative building of evil. She was sure of it. But none of them were to listen. It was Paul's wish to conduct a ritual inside the chapel every third Sunday of the month. They were to carry on with it, no matter how foul of the conditions.

Blood-red roses bloomed in the sunshine from the chapel's stone wall thanks to Bethany's green thumb. Her wisdom in gardening took her way back to when she was a child. She loved to plant. Roses were her favorite, and Paul didn't mind them. Ava saw right through those roses as if they were planted as a disguise for something truly horrific hiding behind these walls.

The nightmare, Ava thought. *Remember the nightmare.*

Her guts felt twisted when they approached the door. It was thick and intimidating. Three strips of metal ran horizontally against the grain. Paul had to give the heavy door a violent nudge to get it to slide open. He reasoned the struggle to be due to the boards swelling in the September heat. That's what made the door so ornery. Every little thing about this chapel had gone wrong so far. Ava sensed the wicked presence of evil inside. And of course, the door was painted the color red.

The chapel was dark inside. So dark, Ava couldn't see Paul even though he stood three feet away. It smelt like a fruit cellar due to the moisture. Ava stepped over the threshold and planted her feet on the wooden floor. As soon as Paul had the candles lit, the chapel suddenly opened up. The walls were plastered in pages from the Holy Bible. Pages upon pages were caked over each other and suspended by small carpenter nails. The flames from three candles flickered off of them. Ava approached the wall and touched the pages. Some of them had warped because of a recent roof leak. The chapel proved to be an ancient alter, indestructible from all kinds of weather. She moved on.

An alter carved from maple stood like a wooden box in the center of the carpeted floor. The carvings told stories from the Old Testament as well as the New Testament. Sketched into the finer sections of the alter was the coming of Christ, the Ten Commandments, a carving of a robust ark towering over a massive body of water, and the crucifixion of Jesus. A deep purple drape with fine craftsmanship trimming surfaced the alter. On it were three candles and the Holy Bible.

Paul knelt as the middle man behind the alter. He had taken his shoes and socks off in the process. He opened the book and tore a page from its binding. With a carpenter nail and a hammer, he pierced the page into the wall behind him. The girls watched from the other side curiously.

As he finished, Ava and Bethany approached the alter. Their bodies were naked and their hair untied. They knelt at the alter while Paul read from *Genesis*. His voice deepened as he read, reciting the text exactly. Ava's eyes wandered around the room, spying on the thousands of pages tacked onto the walls.

This man has finally lost his mind, she thought.

The candles flickered, causing Paul to lose track in his reading. He paused for a moment, located the text with his finger, and began reading again. Ava went from the pages to Bethany's naked body. She had seen it hundreds of Sunday's inside the chapel and it hadn't changed. Bethany's straight blonde scalp turned to coils on her shoulders. Her brown eyes watched Paul as his lips motioned the words. She was smiling.

Ava looked at her own belly. It wasn't much of a belly at all. She admitted of being of victim of a vicious eating disorder for many years but not to this extent. Tears formed in the pits of her eyes when she looked down and saw a shrinking stomach. Her breasts weren't as round as they used to be. The skin practically hung from her skeleton. It sickened her, and she imagined it sickened Paul.

Paul spoke of Adam and Eve and the sin they poisoned the world in. Eve is convinced with the fruit. Adam takes a bite. God finds out and punishes. Ava's heart sunk. Punishment. What a gloomy end to look forward to after life. How would God punish Paul for stealing the lives of other women? Ava found Christianity too troublesome. She refused to believe in it. She laughed at the word punishment. As far as she was concerned, she lived a life of punishment. What kind of God allows that?

Her eyes went to the walls again. She knew the reason behind the pages and why Paul had to nail them to the interior every third Sunday. He was afraid himself of what happens beyond this life. Paul felt insecure and even though he pretended to be what he wasn't, he still led a sinful lifestyle. The pages were covering something up, something he was hiding from them. He was up to no good and Ava was on to him. But confrontation came in the form of a death warrant and only a fool would stand up to Paul's wrath.

That's when Ava noticed something in plain view on Paul's neck. Razor burn sprouts in little bumps. This was something different. That's when it clicked. What if this wasn't a rash at all but evidence left over from a dirty little scum?

It can't be, she thought. Ava looked closer at the mark. *It is!*

The mark began to blister, and it appeared like a scab. But it wasn't a scab. It was a love bruise. Ava knew them as hickeys. The pages from the walls started to come together. What a naughty husband he's been, and she couldn't wait to reveal the hateful truth to Bethany. What a snake!

Paul turned the page and proceeded on with the teachings. Bethany grew wide-eyed like an owl seeking for endless knowledge. Ava looked at her naked body again. Six years in the nude ceased to embarrass her. There was only one word for it. Empowerment. She assumed her nakedness gave Paul some sort of power. And Bethany was too blind to see it regardless of how wide her eyes had gotten.

Paul closed the Bible and tucked it behind the alter. The girls dressed themselves and waited for Paul to relieve the candles of their flame. The chapel went back to sleep in a matter of seconds. Darkness followed. The old fruit cellar odor remained.

The girls headed towards the cabin until Paul said something that caught both of their attention. He was standing under the chapel's awning with the skeleton key in his hand. He dropped it into his pocket and came into the sunlight.

"Early this morning, I walked into my record room and noticed something was out of the ordinary," he said. He stopped and tucked his hands into his front pockets. Ava could tell all kinds of mad was brewing inside that head of his, about ready to explode. His stare locked onto Bethany before it came to Ava. "One of you weren't in there, right?"

Bethany turned to Ava, a dead giveaway. Paul focused on Ava. One of his hands came out from the pocket and took Ava by the shoulder. The grip wasn't aggressive but firm.

"Ava?" he asked. "Are you hiding something from me? You know what happens when you keep secrets. And just think, today is our anniversary. You wouldn't lie to your husband on his anniversary would you? You're not that kind of person."

Ava broke from Paul's grip and started to back away. Fear struck her in every which place, causing her to panic. Breathing felt shallow as she tried to figure a way out from this madness. Bethany wasn't quite sure what was going on except for the fact that Ava did play a Johnny Cash record without notifying Paul about it first.

Ava walked backwards hastily. Paul started to follow.

"I'm sorry Paul," she cried. "I only wanted to listen to music while I dusted. That's all."

"Ava," he said, leading up to her heels. His fingers were spread like claws as he neared. "What have I told you? Rules are rules and now you will be punished for it."

Ava glanced at Bethany with frightened eyes. Tears streamed from her cheeks when she had nothing else to do but run. She got as far as the forest ridge before she felt his body on hers. They landed on the grass in a violent frenzy of rage. Ava screamed as he tore at her dress. The lace loosened as he ripped the cloth into pieces. Baring her breasts, he slapped Ava twice on the face before he cupped his veiny hands on her throat. The nightmare suddenly felt real as he pressed harder on her esophagus, cutting off the air supply completely. Pain erupted in her eyes as her chest tightened.

I'm done for, she thought. *And this time, it's for real.*

She looked into Paul's eyes as her struggle abruptly came close to an end. The pain in her eyes worsened as his strength doubled. She lifted a weak hand to his shoulder but lost all feeling. Her arm fell lifelessly by her side as Bethany ran towards them screaming: *stop it Paul! You're killing her! Stop it!*

Deaf by Bethany's words, he pressed harder. He wanted to hear the snap in her throat, ending all sign of life to this wretched snake. How sinful she's been to disobey the rules! He stared into her dilated eyes as he ground his teeth together.

Ava cocked her head towards Bethany as her mouth made guzzling sounds. She tried to speak but the pressure wouldn't allow it. All Bethany could hear seeping out from Ava's dry mouth was: *aaaaaahhhhhh.*

Bethany jumped onto Paul, forcing him to release his python grip. They collapsed to the grass, leaving Ava bare-breasted in a frightened daze. She coughed and wheezed, begging for air while the two wrestled in the grass. It took one slap in the face for Bethany to quit fighting. He stood from the ground with blood on his lip. He wiped it with his palm and slapped his knee in a fit of rage. He could feel the cold sweats coming on. He looked at Ava, exposed and on the edge of death.

You've gone too far this time pal, he thought. *Any closer, Ava would be dead.*

Bethany crawled to comfort Ava. They cried together while Ava's breathing recovered. A lump of pain clogged her throat as she coughed. Bethany worked on hiding Ava's breasts with the shredded fabric when Paul approached.

"Both of you, inside."

Ignorant to his demand, the girls cried.

"Now!" he shouted.

They fled to the house, Ava against Bethany. When they felt safe, they closed the door and ran upstairs. Paul wiped his bloody lip, tasting the bitterness on his tongue. A storm approached from the North, sending a streak of lightening across an ugly sky.

9

When it rained, it poured.

The storm shook the valley, leaving behind fallen leaves and limbs. The wind swept across the clearing in stages, carrying enormous amounts of rain at an angle. Ava heard it from the bed where she had fallen asleep.

Everything hurt.

The trouble of getting out of bed made her want to lay in the nest of covers forever. She felt a headache coming on. The intense throb pumped to every heart beat. It began somewhere in the middle and made its way to the corners of her eyes. She tried shifting to the other side where she could see the rain drops tint the glass.

Ohhh the pain! God, make it stop.

Her throat felt like she had swallowed a handful of razor blades. She hoped a good nap would have done the trick. But it was no use. The pain was still there, and it was getting worse. Bethany made her rounds by Ava's bedside periodically, checking to make sure everything was fine. When Ava opened her eyes for the first time in the five minutes that transpired, Bethany soothed by the window, listening to the droplets tap the glass.

"Where's Paul?" Ava asked. She crawled to the bedside with her head between her legs. Her head dropped suddenly, weighed down by a painful mass growing inside her cannon ball skull.

"He's downstairs. You should get some more rest."

Ava came to her feet and looked out the window. The rain came to a light mist. The mountains behind the valley were just a blur. Ava had always dreamed of them. What would life be like without Paul? She couldn't imagine how Bethany would react to his death if he'd somehow have an accident. Bethany grew attached to Paul like a fungus. Their relationship led to empty corners of an already darkened room, having no true purpose. Ava questioned if it was the company Paul was after more than a relationship. Perhaps he felt that poor Ava would get lonely when he'd leave Lot. 4-06 everyday for six hours to go venture into the woods alone.

What is so special out there that he has to leave us alone for six hours? she thought.

"What are you doing?" Bethany asked.

"I'm thinking."

"About what?"

Should I really tell her? I mean, is Bethany someone I can really trust in this moment of curiosity? She stared at a trail on the other side of the clearing beside a wooden shed where Paul kept his tools. Only a few yards of trail could be seen from the cabin. As for the rest of it...a mystery.

"Where do you think Paul goes when he leaves the cabin?" Ava asked. Her fingers peeled away small snippets of lime green paint from the windowsill.

Bethany looked curious for a second before she shrugged.

"Hunting the ridge. He's always spotting deer up there."

"He's up to something else."

Bethany stood from the windowsill and stood by Ava's side. They looked out the window together.

"What do you mean?" Bethany asked. She looked at the peeling paint.

"Paul is gone for over six hours a day," Ava said. "What else is he buying time from when he's not hunting?"

"I think your exaggerating Ava. You should really go back to your bed and sleep it off. Your not well after what happened outside."

"You're not thinking logically," Ava said. Her tone darkened. "Bethany, he is gone for six hours. Six hours! Don't you think *that* is a little exaggerated?"

"Okay then," Bethany said. "Let us look at your perspective then. If what you say is true, and he's out there for six hours every day, why is he consistently bringing dead deer home with him?"

"You're in denial."

Bethany cocked her head to the side.

"At first I'm lost. Now, I'm in denial? Just because I don't agree with your far-fetched assumptions, detective, doesn't mean that I've lost touch with reality. Why don't you get back into bed--"

"Stop saying that!" Ava shouted.

They paused for a moment to listen for any sign of movement downstairs.

"What is it that you want Ava? I mean, what are you looking for that I'm apparently not aware of?"

Ava turned towards the windowsill again and looked at the trail.

"There's something else isn't there?" Bethany asked. "Something you're not telling me."

Ava sighed.

"What is it? Tell me, please. You and I have never kept anything secretive from ourselves. What is it?"

"I saw a mark," Ava said. "It was on his neck. A love bite."

"What?" Bethany said, confused. "I didn't do that."

"And neither did I," Ava said.

"Then who did?"

Ava shook her head and looked out the window again. Bethany brought her hand to her cheek and started towards Ava's bed where she had to stop and think for a moment. Ava stood by the window with her hands on the peeling paint.

"Why don't you take a break from the outside world for a change," Bethany told Ava. "You act like you're entitled to it. Why don't you just face the music. You're not going anywhere."

Silence.

"Ava?"

Nothing.

Bethany returned to the window to find Ava in a daze.

"What is so interesting out there?" Bethany asked.

"Paul's trail is beside the shed," Ava said. "The one he walks each day."

Bethany had to see it for herself. The narrow trail was tucked to the right corner of the wooden shed and enclosed by a cluster of oak trees. It looked like a little hole a groundhog would call his entrance.

"You're not suggesting that we--"

Ava nodded her head before Bethany had time to finish her sentence.

"No," Bethany said. "Absolutely not. Don't you remember what he did to you outside the chapel over a record. He almost killed you. I'm not going along with it. You can't make me."

"Bethany, he exposed me," Ava said. She felt hurt by saying it. "Do you know what that feels like to be ripped at and exposed? You're right Bethany. He hurt me. Isn't that enough to justify?"

Bethany shook her head again, crossed her arms, and walked across the room. She stared towards the two beds. A pine branch scraped at the window between the beds, making an awful scratching noise.

"I am not doing it Ava," she said. "You are taking it too far this time, you know. Too far."

Ava crossed the floor and crawled beside Bethany with her hands on her shoulder.

"Do this for me Bethany," she said. "We have to know for ourselves."

"You know something's wrong," Ava said. "You're just not admitting to it. Come with me. If we get halfway and you don't want to go any further, we'll come back."

Bethany shook her head again but Ava knew her well enough to see the spark in her eyes. She's curious.

"What if you're right," Bethany said. "What can we do about it? Nothing. You dig deep enough you're going to find bones."

"Assurance," Ava said. "At least, we wouldn't be left out not knowing what was going on."

"If he finds out about this," Bethany said. "You know quite well what he will do to us."

"We run the risk."

"It's too great of a risk."

Silence again.

"For years, we've been doing the same thing over and over again," Ava said. "We've obeyed his rules for the most part. We've cooked his meals and cleaned his house. You and I are getting older. What do you think will happen when he doesn't want us anymore?"

Bethany thought about it for a moment before she took Ava's hand.

"I will do this for you," she said. "But if something goes wrong, we run straight back. Got it?"

Ava nodded.

"Paul is going to wake up soon for supper," she said. "You should probably say something to him. It's your anniversary, and he wants to spend it with you tonight. It's probably best to make up now or he'll get rough, understand?"

Ava broke into tears again but Bethany was right.

"Promise me you will do that," Bethany asked. "Promise me."

Ava wiped her tears away and held onto Bethany.

"I promise."

10

Supper had come and gone with as little hassle as possible.

Bethany got stuck with the dishes while Paul arranged a nice dance with Ava to the sound of Bob Dylan on acoustic guitar. The lights in the open space of the downstairs were dimmed while they danced. Shelves upon shelves of books stood around them watching their moves. A deer head protruded from the West wall between two book shelves. His beady eyes served as a reflection of their backwards world.

Paul shifted his feet as he held her waist. His breath chilled her neck as he guided her along the floor in basic motions. While they danced, Ava looked at the shelves of books. There were so many. Stories of a giant squid, the great hunt for a whale, and Boy Scouts lost on an island. Her favorite novel from Paul's book collection was Joseph Heller's *Catch-22*.

"There's something I've been wanting to tell you," Paul said. He spun her around and brought her back to his chest. The lights circled and spun around her making her feel dizzy inside.

"What is it?"

"I want to apologize for the little act we had outside this morning," he said. "It wasn't right for me to do what I did. But next time, you must ask me first before rooting through my records."

"I understand Paul. You're forgiven."

"I know how I get sometimes. It's not easy for you girls, especially on Chapel Sunday. I want you to be aware that I am pleased with your company. You and Bethany are all I have in this world."

She heard those words fade as the music came to a close.

You and Bethany are all I have in this world...

In this world...

In this world...

In this world...

11

Morning crept up on Ava when she woke up with a stitch in her side. The pain felt too great at first but when she moved to the bedside, it was only the beginning.

Ahhh!

Ava cupped her stomach, in need of a medic. Something wasn't quite right here. Something she couldn't fix. And it wasn't leaving anytime soon. Ava threw the sweat-stained covers away and took a series of deep breaths. Her intestines felt like they were a knotted up snake. The air became thick and bitter around her. Not helping.

Ava tried moving again, crying when she couldn't even stand. The agony originated at the core of her belly and radiated through her anal canal. She felt torn inside as if a butcher wrecked havoc there. She looked at the bedroom door, praying it would open by itself so she could crawl on the floor. Paul and Bethany were downstairs.

I could scream. Yes, that is a good plan. But what will I do if they can't hear me? I'm sure my voice won't last beyond the staircase. Oh, no. I'll be stuck here all morning before someone will notice I'm missing. Stuck here in agonizing pain!

Ava dug her fingers into the bedpost as she suffered. All she could think about was the night before when Paul started kissing her neck. Everything was fine up until he started getting rough with her.

Once a solid five minutes elapsed, it wasn't so bad. She could stand, at least. But walking was tough when a fuzzy migraine began to grow. She walked the path of golden sunshine to the door and paused. The migraine throbbed and poked watery blotch marks in her vision.

Slow it down Ava. Slow it down.

She took smaller strides down the hallway and towards the stairs. The pain in her back diminished but the migraine refused. It was there to stay.

Bethany worked at the sink basin, peeling the skins off granny apples with a knife. She'd peel an apple and drop them into a bowl for dicing. Ava stumbled into the kitchen, giving Bethany quite a scare. She laid the knife beside the apple bowl, gave her hands a swift dry on the towel tied around her waist, and came to Ava's aid.

"What's wrong?" Bethany asked. She guided Ava to a chair by the table. The fragrance of dusting liquid lingered as Bethany brought up a chair for herself. "You look like you're in pain."

You have no idea, Ava thought.

"I ache everywhere."

"Do you need anything?" Bethany asked. "You just tell me and I'll be on it. Promise."

Ava shifted to the left, hoping her tailbone would sit nicely on the sunflower cushion. The sunshine snuck through every window in the cabin, illuminating the inside up in a blaze of golden light. Almost too bright for the human eyes to bare, Ava closed hers to prevent an atomic bomb from detonating inside her hurting skull. Grains of plastic rice scattered across her vision like wiggling larvae in a cluster. The dusting polish scent was at its smelliest now as the sun's heat rested on the wooden table.

"I'll be fine for now," she said.

"Where does it hurt?"

Where doesn't it hurt?

"My head feels like it's about ready to pop," Ava said.

Ava slouched in the chair feeling troubled. All of the pains in the world seemed to come crashing down on her as if gravity had a grudge. Bethany left her seat to fetch Ava a cold ice rag from the counter. She folded the rag and placed it horizontally across Ava's burning forehead. Ava soothed as the chill worked on scaring the pain away for good. Bethany returned to her chair and watched the clouds darken the trees.

"Did you sleep well?" Bethany asked.

Ava repositioned the rag to get the full dose of chill.

"Not at all," Ava said. "He was rough last night."

"Rough like how?" Bethany asked.

Ava looked around the downstairs.

"Where's Paul?"

"Outside."

"Doing what?"

"Sharpening his ax for firewood," Bethany said. "He's been at it all morning ever since he woke up. I see he left you oversleep."

Ava closed her eyes again and sighed.

"He told me he wanted to try something new and I permitted it," Ava said. "As you can see now, I'm regretting it."

"Was it the missionary position?"

"I'm not that lucky," Ava told Bethany. "He hammered me from behind and when I say behind, that's where he ended up."

"I'm sorry," Bethany said, feeling guilty about the reaction. "I had no idea he was going to—"

"He did."

The throbbing in her back started again as soon as Ava stood up. She wanted to scream. She wanted something to alleviate the pain. She wanted out. Bethany stood and held Ava for a while. Ava buried her face into Bethany's shoulder and wept. The vibrations from Ava's crying spell sent a spasm down Bethany's diaphragm. When Ava was finished, she sniffed and wiped her eyes.

"Have you eaten?" Bethany asked.

"I haven't this morning," Ava said, wiping her palm under her wet nose. "I've been doing this ever since I woke up."

Bethany reached for a freshly peeled apple and handed one off to Ava. Ava took it and nibbled at the tasty flesh. Bethany watched Ava as she ate, troubled by the fact that Ava had the illness for quite some time. When Ava was finished with the apple, she handed the rest to Bethany.

"You're scaring me Ava."

Ava sniffed again.

"How so?"

"With this," Bethany said, holding the apple between them. "I count three full bites. This isn't enough to keep you alive. In fact, you ought to be dead by the way you pick at your food. It's not healthy."

"What is anymore?" Ava asked. She went back to her chair to stare out the window. "I still want to do it Beth. Even all the pain in the world isn't going to stop me from walking those woods. You know that."

"I know," Bethany said, curling her hands beneath her towel. "Determination can be a strong thing sometimes."

Bethany stood behind Ava's chair. They looked at the woods together.

"I know how important this is to you," Bethany said. "That's why I'm willing to keep my promises. But I've decided I'm not going with you."

Ava turned.

"What do you mean?"

"Ava, someone has to stay behind just in case something goes wrong. I'll stand by you till we get to White Rock. After that, you are on your own."

Bethany left Ava at the table to dice the apples by the sink. Ava managed to sneak in some thoughts about the trail before she approached the counter. A bundle of granny apples were already peeled, waiting to be diced by the blade of Bethany's eager knife. As she worked the knife blindly, using muscle memory to finish the job, she entertained herself by staring outside the kitchen window. The back of Lot. 4-06 was nothing but more woodlands. An occasional deer could be seen from the window but anything else was simply staring off into oblivion.

"Can I ask you a question Ava?" Bethany asked. She dropped a fresh handful of apple blocks into an empty bowl.

"Anything."

"In the past five years I've been living here at Lot. 4-06, I've noticed you've shown a minimal appreciation for God. Why is that?"

Ava noticed Bethany had broken her concentration from the backyard woodland and had locked eyes on Ava. The density in her eyes revealed the seriousness of the question. Ava had no choice but to deliver her answer in its truest form.

"I don't buy into this God business," Ava said. "For six years, I've prayed something would happen to Paul. That way, I wouldn't have to worry about stepping on glass all the time, abusing my body would be the thing of the past, and I could do anything I want. You don't need God to do that. He's nothing but an illusion. A figment of your imagination."

Bethany stopped her cutting and wiped the blade clean with the towel.

"You're accusing me that I'm lost all the time which is fine," Bethany said. "Did it ever occur to you that maybe you're the one whose lost? Paul orders you to not keep him waiting and you respond in an instant. But yet, you keep God waiting."

Lost for words, Ava walked away leaving Bethany behind to finish her dicing.

12

Ava insisted she would lead the way, and Bethany would follow only because she knew the woods more than anyone else around. They started by the shed and worked their way into the depths of darkness. The temperature felt cooler under the shade. The ground was moist from the underground springs which carried the water from the top of the mountain to the bottom of the valley. Bethany could hear the water sliding between the rocks beneath all the leafy debris.

The journey worried Bethany because Paul was not an idiot by any means. He knew the woods just as much as Ava did, and he knew how to track. She looked at Ava's foot prints in the muddy floor and realized just how obvious it was.

"He's going to kill us when he finds out about this," Bethany said.

Ava took a tree limb and pushed it aside for them to pass.

"He won't find out."

"How much of that are you certain?" Bethany asked. Ava sensed the dread in her voice.

"I don't."

"We should go back," Bethany cried. "I can't do this anymore. Let's go back."

Ava stopped by a mossy stump and grabbed Bethany by the shoulders. Both of them breathed heavily.

"Stop it Bethany," she said. "Just, stop it. Everything will be alright. Paul will not find out about this, I promise. You will get yourself worked up over nothing, and it will spoil our plan. Got it?"

Ava refused to accept Bethany's opinion on the matter. Although Ava remembered Bethany's promise she made in the living room, she started to feel this sudden urge of self-doubt beginning to overcome Beth and her ability to follow this through. Denying it would only make her angry and anger wasn't something Ava needed at the moment. In fact, she wished Bethany would have stayed at home which would have relieved her the excess baggage.

Fifteen minutes elapsed which seemed like hours. Ava stuck to the trail before it's muddy floor turned to solid rock. The walking came easier regardless of the achy bones from the night before. The pain in her lower back faded overtime, but there was no denying that it wasn't still there. She hoisted her torso over the backbone of the rocks and waited.

Geese flocked over her in their V formation, heading South towards the marshes over yonder. Ava counted eight geese. Four on the right wing and three on the other. They honked, locking their wings in the process. The landing would take place another hundred yards causing Ava to lose complete sight of the geese. But she was aware of the pond's forbidden location. She's been there before.

Bethany choked on the miserable insects as she pulled herself up from the thorny bushes. Both her arm and knee were scratched, dripping with blood. They stood on the spine of the trail and looked forward where the trees bowed inward, creating a tunnel. Light broke through the dripping wet canopy and snuck into the tunnel, illuminating their path littered with needles and acorns. Bethany went for Ava's hand as they walked through, listening carefully to the dreadful silence. Sticks cracked in the great beyond, giving Bethany quite a scare.

Ava's hand went numb when they exited the tunnel and into the open. The air smelt different. A wall of pines stood tall ahead of them, peering down like green giants. The trail kept going like a never ending snake. Ava had visited many places beyond the marked trails, but this was something she had never seen before. A red streak of paint scarred the trunk from one of the pines, signifying its forbidden state. Ava brushed her fingertips over the streak and noticed there were hundreds more. Paul had given this prohibited place a name.

The boundary.

"This isn't what I think it is, is it?" Bethany asked. She stood behind Ava with her eyes on the red mark.

"It's the boundary," Ava whispered, feeling the bark nip at her flesh.

A white rock protruded from the ground outside the boundary where Bethany made herself comfortable. She watched Ava gaze at the wall of trees in aspiring triumph. Nothing in this realm could produce enough strength to rob Ava of this aspiration. Nothing at all.

"We did it Beth," Ava said. "I can't believe we reached it."

Bethany swiveled on the white rock and looked at the boundary. The wail of a Common Loon broke the silence as a cicada shook his rattle in a nearby tree. The wind grew heavy again and rocked the trees.

"I don't like this," Bethany said. She stood from the rock and backed away. "The sounds."

"You're over reacting again," Ava said. "It's just a Loon."

"It's evil," Bethany said. "Don't you get it? Maybe there is a good reason why Paul kept us on this side for all these years. There's something about this I don't like Ava."

"It's metaphorical," Ava said. "Paul crosses it every day. Alright, look. If you don't want to continue with me, you can find your way back on your own as you've made clear back at the cabin. I'm not going back until I find out what Paul's been up to. I'm not scared of a little old wives' tale that Paul's been spoon feeding us for years. He's scaring you to prevent you from going past this. Nothing supernatural is going on here. It's all in your head."

Bethany's eyes dropped.

"I'm sorry Ava," she said. "This is where I leave you. I've kept my word to go no further than the White Rock."

"You did," Ava replied. "I can't ask much more than that."

"You're really going to do this then?"

"I'm destined to," Ava said.

Ava had one foot in when she felt Bethany's tighten around her waist.

"Be safe in there," Bethany said. "Then come back to me."

13

A thunderstorm came in from the East and shook the mountain when the thunder rumbled. Streaks of lightening split the sky while violent winds sent the woods into a whirlpool of craziness. Bethany lacked the courage Ava portrayed and decided enough was enough and headed back towards the cabin. Bethany ascended alone, far and wide, back to where she started. When she reached the shed, the sky grew dark and alarming.

A sudden flash of lightening broke apart the sky followed by thunder.

Crack!

Bethany ran to the porch and threw open the door. She lit three candles by the table where she sat close to the overlook window. The wind had really started to pick up, thrashing the trees against one another. The whole forest looked like a battle ring. She kept the candles close as she reached for one of the records Paul had accidentally left out. So unlike him.

She took the disc and snapped it into the wooden record player. Resting the needle on the vinyl surface, Bethany closed her eyes and listened to the Zombies sing their *Time of the Season.*

14

Six years earlier...

Ava used to live in a small ranch home with her mother for eighteen years outside of a small town in Pennsylvania. The name of the town as well as its exact whereabouts escaped Ava's memory because Paul had relocated her after eighteen years of living with her mother. Life was good back home. Mother was god's gift, and Ava had learned a lot from her. But as soon as she reached the age of eighteen, some man she had never seen before told her that she was going away for a while. No questions. She was ordered to pack a bag of clothes and wish her mother farewell. She asked when she'd be able to see her mother again. The answer was, never.

The man who had stolen Ava from her mother's home was a beefy middle aged man who wore tucked in checkered flannels inside his darkened denim. He wore a beard down to his chest pockets and smoked like a chimney using filtered cigarettes. Where these cigarettes or clothes come from remained a mystery to poor Ava who had lived a sheltered life for eighteen years. Then suddenly, those eighteen years no longer mattered. She was taken away by the bearded stranger who had worked a family agreement with the mother before packing her away inside some rusty old dodge truck. Her head was covered beneath seed sack which was a terrible idea considering she could see right through the blurry squares that held the sack together. She had a good memory of where the roads had taken her up until six years of forgetfulness kicked in.

Ava went twenty minutes before he removed the seed sack.

He brought a cracked fingernail to his chapped lips as he whispered, "Don't be afraid. Everything will make sense here shortly but for now, I need you to stay quiet and do everything I say. Don't make a fuss either. We don't want that. Do you understand everything I just told you?"

Although nothing made any sense to her, she nodded. What she wanted to tell the man was that she missed her mother terribly and wanted to go back. But not knowing what the man was capable of doing, she took the man's advice and kept her lips sealed.

"That's a good girl," he told her, feeling her hair fall between his fingers.

He opened her door, revealing a long rectangular cabin in the distance. The man walked her towards the front porch where two younger girls smiled and waved. Ava refused to communicate with the girls, even though they provoked her. They simply stared and giggled against one another with their dresses in the dirt. The man with chapped lips yelled something offensive at the girls which motivated them to carry on with their chores.

The cabin reminded Ava of a shack with windows and a porch. It had two stories and provided plenty of rooms. The man gripped Ava at the wrists and directed her to the front door. Nailed to the right of the door was a sign that had the following inscription carved into it: Lot. 1-04. The man guided her in.

The cabin smelt of burnt wood and cheese. Twenty women in white gowns gathered around Ava while the man brought her a glass of lemonade. He sat across the table from Ava and pushed the glass towards her.

"Where am I?" Ava asked, taking a sip from the glass. It was sour.

"The name is George, and the girls who are standing around me are your sisters."

Ready to choke on the sour drink, she pushed the glass aside.

"Sisters?"

"That's right," he said. He reached for Ava's glass and took a drink himself, cringing at the sour taste. "All twenty of them."

Twenty, she thought. *Oh good heavens!*

"I will answer any questions that you may have," George said.

"Why am I here?" she asked, thinking of mother.

The girls surrounding George were twisting their hair and giggling quietly amongst themselves. Some of them were older than others but still young.

"You are here because you are born into a family that practices polygamy. Do you know what that is Ava?"

She didn't.

"You will live in the boarding house until I appoint you a husband. Now, this could take weeks, months, even years. However, until your future husband arrives, you will live here and abide by our rules."

"Rules?"

"Yes, rules," George replied. "There are seven of them, but we will get to that eventually. For now, you will be shown to a bed so you can settle down. Before we get to that, do you have more questions for me?"

"I'll never get to see my mother again, will I?"

George sighed.

"This is your home now," he said. "There is nothing new going on to you that hasn't happened to any of these girls already. Every female goes through the same cycle in life on their eighteenth birthday. This isn't personal. It's just something that this family has been involved in for many years. Questions?"

Ava shook her head when George stood.

"Well then," he said. "Welcome to the boarding house."

15

For several months, the boarding house became the new way of life. Gospel teachings of Jesus Christ were taught in small numbers by older sisters of the family, ones who were seasoned enough to understand the Holy Bible in its entirety.

Days consisted of strict chores and discipline: how to clean floors, dishes, and the laundry. Other days consisted of how to please sexually. These teachings consisted of sexual practices that were demonstrated to the group. Ava was chosen by the lead sisters to demonstrate the sexual positions that were appropriate for direct penetration. Medical anatomy went as far as what the internal structure of both genitals and genitalia look like. Then, the specifications on preparing for children.

The most important lesson taught by the lead sisters was how to obey your husbands rules. These rules were universal and were never to be crossed. In order for the younger girls to understand what the rules meant, they were forced to write them every morning, evening, and before they went to bed. There were seven of them: 1) Never cross the boundary, 2) Suicidal feelings or thoughts alone are forbidden, 3) Obey your husband, 4) The chapel and its rituals are sacred, 5) Beware of secrets for they are cancerous, 6) Chores are strict and performed every day, and 7) A woman's killing is not justified.

A sample of the writing would appear as follows:

Never cross the boundary. Suicidal feelings or thoughts alone are forbidden. Obey your husband. The chapel and its rituals are sacred. Beware of secrets for they are cancerous. Chores are strict and performed every day. A woman's killing is not justified. Never cross the boundary. Suicidal feelings or thoughts alone are forbidden. Obey your husband. The chapel and its rituals are sacred. Beware of secrets for they are cancerous. Chores are strict and performed every day. A woman's killing is not justified. Never cross the boundary. Suicidal feelings or thoughts alone are forbidden. Obey your husband. The chapel and its rituals are sacred. Beware of secrets for they are cancerous. Chores are strict and performed every day. A woman's killing is not justified. Never cross the boundary. Suicidal feelings or thoughts alone are forbidden. Obey your husband. The chapel and its rituals are sacred. Beware of secrets for they are cancerous. Chores are strict and performed every day. A woman's killing is not justified.

The sisters took their rule writing very seriously, and if one would happen to deviate from the structure, misspell, or obscure the writing in any way, the sister would have to endure the other end of Deborah's belt.

Deborah was one of the eldest who loved inflicting damage to the flesh. The redder the better was her motto and the words practically gushed from her mouth every time she'd bring the belt around to the bare skin. Better yet, she'd butter the leather belt with water before the torture would begin. This made the pain live there a little longer before it would eventually pass.

Ava could only remember suffering at the end of Deborah's venomous serpent once in the three months she spent at the boarding house. The incident occurred inside the boarding house chapel which was a small building three yards from the cabin. The chapel served as a model for the real deal and was completely bare inside. Ava was supposed to undress for the ritual and when she refused, her clothes were torn at the seams and her bottom raked with burns. She cried for a week, hoping the burn would subside. Nothing prevailed. It took several bags of ice to cool that sucker down before it even came close to healing.

Paul was invited to the house for his appointment. That's where the introduction took place. It was love at first sight. And once Paul set his eyes on Ava, he made the conversation with George a quick one and married her at his chapel.

16

A clash of thunder radiated from the sky and made the cabin tremble. Bethany finished polishing the book shelves when the rain started to get heavier. She heard it on the roof and saw it forming ponds in the middle of the clearing. Rivers were being made as the water gnawed through the dirt and mud, completely eroding the soil away from the roots in the yard. Some of Bethany's roses by the chapel failed to make it out alive.

The sky continued to darken like a cloak being flung over the mountains by an unforgiving God. She watched from the window as a strike of lightening separated the darkness. She was ready to close the curtain again until the front door flew open.

It was Ava drenched in rain.

"Don't scare me like that," Bethany said, feeling her heart pounding in her chest.

Before Bethany had a chance to tend to the wet clothes, Ava had already taken the initiative by flapping the wet dress off her skeleton. She carried the clothes to the sink basin where she dropped them.

"Did you find Paul?" Bethany asked.

Ava shivered while she sought for a dry towel. When she found one, she ran her hair through it.

"No."

"Did he find you?"

"Of course not," Ava said. She flipped the towel to the other side and continued drying.

"Did you find anything then?"

Ava threw the towel into the sink, carelessly not thinking. Bethany retrieved the clothes and stuck them with the wet ones beside the wood stove. Ava walked upstairs in her underwear to change while Bethany waited by the window. Upon Ava's return, Bethany pried again.

"You found something, didn't you?" Bethany asked.

"I did," she replied. "And its best if I don't tell you."

"Come on," Bethany continued, quite irritated with Ava's response. "If it was you who stayed cooped up in the cabin while I was out looking, you'd want to know what I had found."

Ava turned her head away and shook her head.

"Not true," Ava said.

"It is," Bethany replied. "And it must be pretty interesting if you're not telling me. But if you can't bring yourself around and tell me what you found, so be it. I'll be upstairs."

And Bethany was well on her way until she heard Ava say her name. Bethany stopped by the staircase and turned around to find Ava staring back at her.

"What is it?"

"You really want to know what I found?" Ava asked. "Even if it might upset you?"

"Try me."

Ava paused, thinking of all the ways this could turn ugly. She worried about Bethany. It was the truth, but revealing what she had found on her travels was something Ava would soon regret. That's when she decided to come clean with it.

"I found the boarding house."

17

They shared dinner together in silence.

Paul went for the ham and downed his bottle of wine. His wedding ring was gold, and it would glimmer every time the light touched it. Both Ava and Bethany were given silver wedding bands. Bethany's ring was in much better condition than Ava's only because she took care of it. Ava could have cared less about its condition. Sometimes, she wished she'd throw it in the stream every time she'd visit it. Hook, line, and sinker.

Ava walked her plate to the counter when they finished dinner. The squash and slices of apple were still there untouched. The waste basket ate up most of her food over the years. No remorse came over her as she'd watch their hard earned food go right into the trash.

Paul sent them upstairs after kissing them both on the cheek. He stayed downstairs as they dressed into their night gowns and slipped into their beds. It was a full moon that night.

Johnny Cash's voice filled the hall with *Daddy Sang Bass* when Ava closed her eyes. Having been her favorite since a little girl, she lipped the words silently to herself. Meanwhile, Bethany turned over beneath her covers and stared at Ava's back.

"He knows, doesn't he?" Bethany whispered. "He knows what we've done."

Ava turned to face Bethany.

"How do you know that?"

"He never listens to Johnny Cash," Bethany said. "Think back to when you walked through the woods earlier today. Did you leave anything behind? Tracks? Anything at all that would make him suspicious?"

"No," she replied. "Nothing I can think of. Maybe you're reading the wrong signals."

"I don't think so," Bethany replied, pulling the cold covers to her chin.

Where do I begin? Bethany thought. *Of all things to stumble upon in the woods, she finds the one thing that haunts any woman who lived within its walls. How could Paul not tell us! We were living under a blanket for years without knowing how close we really were to it.*

"How close did you get to it?" Bethany asked.

"I didn't go walking in if that's what you're asking."

"Then how could you be so sure that it wasn't another cabin?" Bethany said. "Maybe it was a different cabin that made you remember. Could that be a possibility?"

"I saw it Bethany," Ava said. "It looks exactly like it did six years ago when I was boarded there."

Bethany wanted to curl beneath the covers and cry herself to sleep. Instead, she stared at Ava. She wanted some kind of truth to this story so it could debunk what Ava had seen.

"You've never told me what you've experienced there," Ava said. "Would you mind telling me?"

Bethany sighed.

"I was boarded five years ago," she said. "Three months into the extensive training, I was ridiculed and laughed at because of my weight. I wasn't like the other girls. I wasn't fat neither, just a little chubby around the waist. Before I was introduced to Paul, I remember being beaten by the sisters at night while George was asleep."

"Why haven't you told me about this Bethany?" Ava said. "They abused you."

"The sisters never liked me. Thought of me as a different breed. A minute wouldn't go by without somebody either laughing at me or putting their foot out across the crowded walkway during lectures so they could laugh at me after I'd trip. They did all sorts of bullying. My hair was pulled, my clothes were torn, my name would change, and they'd laugh. Deb was in on it too. They'd prank me into doing things I wasn't suppose to, only looking for an excuse to get Deborah in with that belt."

"How often would she whip you?" Ava asked.

Bethany took a second to remember an estimate.

"I'd say a couple times every day."

"Heavens," Ava said, shaking her head. "I'm sorry Beth. I had no idea or I would have never asked."

"There's something else," Bethany said. "Something I've kept secret from everybody, even Paul."

Ava threw the covers across the bed and accompanied Bethany's side.

"What is it?" Ava asked.

Bethany had burst into tears. An upsetting series of events took place on Bethany's face when she went from being alright to abnormal. Tears streamed from her eyes and dripped from her chin as she rested her head on Ava's breast. Ava comforted her, hoping the story would come out. Bethany cried for a few minutes before she was ready to bury her soul.

"Ava," she said, sniffing. "You are all I have left in this world. You've always been there for me. Please promise me you'll keep this between us. Every word I've told you will never leave this room. Even in rage."

"You have my word," Ava said. Bethany wiped her eyes and looked at the full moon outside their window.

"George had these walks back at the boarding house," she said. "He was quite fond of them, normally requesting that I'd go with him a couple days out of the week. We'd walk alone. Sometimes we wouldn't stray too far from the house. But on certain occasions, he'd take me further until we were far enough nobody could see us. He'd take my gown off and kiss me a little. Then, we'd spend time touching each other. He told me we wouldn't go back until..."

"I'm sorry Beth," Ava said. "Did he ever have intercourse with you?"

"No," Bethany said. "He may have been an arrogant pervert, but he knew the family rules that only the husbands were permitted to break virginity. George somehow knew I'd keep my mouth shut as long as he'd keep the sisters off my back. I felt trapped Ava."

"You must have been depressed."

"No Ava," Bethany said. "Not when you have faith to keep you occupied. The sisters may have broken me down. George may have had his way with me. But when you have faith, nothing can take that away. I've learned to forgive."

"Must he hard," Ava said. "To forgive I mean. All the life shattering experiences you've lived with for all these years."

"It is hard," Bethany said. "I won't lie."

When Bethany had enough for one night, Ava went back to her bed and thought about the delicate conversation Bethany had shared with her. A range of mixed feelings about this whole family business swept through Ava like madness. Now, she wanted out forever. But planing an escape was not so easy especially when one of them still had strong feelings for Paul. She turned to face Bethany who had already fallen asleep. She looked at the cracked door where the hallway light crept into their bedroom.

Don't you worry Beth, Ava thought. *One way or another, you and I will be free from this place. I promise you that much.*

She laid there in the darkness with only Johnny, June, and the light from the crack in the door to carry her off to sleep.

18

Bethany was picking blueberries from the side garden the following morning when Paul decided to chop some firewood. At each swing with the ax, two pieces of wood would fly off the block. He had a pretty reasonable stack along the cabin, narrowing the top out to form a triangle. The pieces lined up along the bottom used to be rotten due to moisture. To put a fix to the problem once and for all, Paul waited until all of the wood was burned, applied a row of cylinder block as a base, and started a new stack. Since then, his idea worked.

Paul swung the ax, slicing a log in two. Planting the blade of the ax into solid ground, he wiped the sweat away from his brow and watched Bethany pick her berries. Mosquitoes were getting bad which often brought undesired welts and pus. Nobody liked bumps on their arms especially itchy ones. He waved his hand inches from his face. A nearby swamp proved to be a breeding ground for the buggers.

Feeling his heart beating rapidly in his chest from the exhaustion of the craft, he took a break by the cabin. He watched Bethany reach for the berries, occasionally scanning a few before giving the rotten ones a swift toss to the grass. Gardening was her sanctuary—a modest place for her to get away from the world for a little while. But was it really working? After slapping his sweaty neck, finally squashing the pest in his palm, he approached the garden.

The garden wasn't big at all for it only covered about twenty feet in each direction. It was a dirt square full of melons, berries, and vegetables. Half of the garden was exposed to the sun while the remainder waited patiently for its turn for some evening sunshine.

Bethany kept to her business, making sure each berry was pulp enough to give the tongue a sour teaser. When the picking was done alone, she'd sneak a few berries into her mouth.

"How's the picking?"

Bethany jumped, dropping a few berries on the ground. *No!* she thought, picking up the berries. Worried that he might get offended, she stuffed them into the basket and looked up to him like a dog that had wet the bed. He towered over her with the sun behind him. His eyes were demanding, fishing for answers. The sweat rolled down his forehead and off his nose, dripping carelessly into the grass in front of her. The weight of his wet hair hung by his shoulders like the hair of a witch.

Paul knelt in front of the basket, pinched a blueberry between his fingers, and bit down on its sourly substance.

"Is there something you and Ava are not telling me?" he asked, tilting his head.

"What gives you that idea?" she said.

He took another blueberry.

He knows, she thought. *The panic! The horror!*

"The both of you have been acting very strange in the past few days," he said. "Especially you, Bethany. Are you sure there is nothing you want to tell me? You are fully aware of the rules, aren't you? You wouldn't be that wife who hides things from their husbands certainly not."

"There's nothing in this world I would hide from you Paul," she said.

It was a lie.

She lied about everything. She looked at the porch over Paul's shoulder, hoping Ava would come to her rescue. But what Ava really needed was luck. Paul squeezed a blueberry and wiped the guts on his pants.

"This isn't an abstract question," he said. "Use that stupid brain of yours and tell me what is going on between the two of you."

Her eyes met the blueberry stain on his pants.

"I..."

She couldn't breathe. When she went to say something, all she could think about was Ava lying on the ground by the chapel with her clothes ripped apart. Now, she sensed she'd get the same treatment, maybe worse.

"Bethany," he said. "You're testing my patience."

Her hand left the basket and hid beneath the apron. A wasp nest dangled from off a small ledge on the shed. Bethany had inched her way towards it where five stinging-eager wasps circled their hive. One flew off when Paul lifted a hand and slapped Bethany across the face, unleashing a storm of pain. First, the numb feeling. Then, the real pain began. Her balance caved causing her to fall back on the shed, crushing the wasp nest. Not only did she have a raving lunatic of a husband hungry for more pain, she also had a family of angry wasps after her.

"You stupid cow," he shouted. "Stupid, stupid cow."

Bethany brought her legs towards her chest, cupping the hurting side of her face. Trapped within the confines of the shed, Paul found a perfect opportunity to inflict more damage. With nowhere to go, Bethany prepared for the worst.

Most of the wasps had given up while two of them had yet to retire. Paul darkened the corner with his massive body. He batted at the wasp, successfully dispatching it. Bethany shielded her face with both hands, hoping Paul would come to his senses. Instead, Paul squeezed himself into the confined area and threw as many punches her way as he could. Bethany screamed, losing breaths in between each blow. It took a moment before Paul grew tired from the abuse. He threw his wet hair over his scalp and wiped the blood on his pants.

Bethany felt relieved that the flare outlived its course. She concentrated on the pain in her chest where the final punch knocked the wind out of her. Blood drizzled from her lower lip where it swelled. The more she sucked, the thicker it got.

Paul went back to chopping his wood when Bethany found her footing. She carried the basket to the porch, keeping an eye on Paul just in case he was thirsty for more. He never came back but needless to say, he was very unpredictable. She left the basket by the door and found Ava attending to the dishes. She rushed to the basin and dabbed her swollen lip.

"What happened!" Ava said. She dabbed a wash rag on the wound. "You're bleeding like a stuck pig."

"He knows something is up," Bethany said.

"What do you mean he knows?" Ava asked.

"He knows we are up to no good. I don't want you going to that place anymore. This is getting too dangerous."

"You're talking about crossing the boundary?" Ava asked. She applied more pressure to the cut causing Bethany to cringe.

"Yes," Bethany said. "I don't know how he knows but he suspects something is going on. You know how he gets when something is off."

"I know."

"If you know then you will promise me you won't do it again."

Ava nodded.

"I won't cross the boundary anymore," Ava said. "If that makes you happy."

"It doesn't only make me happy," Bethany said, throwing the rag on the counter. "It keeps me alive."

19

The rise of a crimson sun almost changed Ava's mind while she stood thinking beside the ferns. A rotten sun in the morning seemed out of place like something was bound to go wrong. A perfect setup. Should I be doing this or should I just forget it? That's where Ava was in the game. What's the worth of a promise? Promises get broken every day, don't they? She gazed at the ferns again. So green. So wet. Several yards over the ferns was the same trail Ava had taken the day before. The trail where

Paul did his dirty work on the other side. She considered the promise she shared with Bethany, thought about it some more, and then made her decision. She decided to go for it.

Why?

The reason on her behalf was really quite simple. The hours she spent spying on Paul the last few days became bothersome. Something serious was at work. Paul worked on making a wooden frame in the backyard. The project's estimated due date ended up putting him back a day or so, making him a real bear to deal with later. That's when Bethany got caught in one of his flares. And while they were busy duking it out by the shed and disturbing the wasp nest, Ava had her wet hands on the dishes and her eyes on the frame covered by the tarp. At first, she wondered what it was. Then, she knew.

It's a bed frame.

But for whom?

The crazy idea kept her guessing. Maybe one of their beds needed replacing. Maybe not.

Mosquitoes at their finest swarmed around her sweaty forehead, keeping watch with their beady eyes hoping to catch a break so they could sneak their splinters into her flesh. Some of the winged pests managed to leave behind a trail of welts on her arms, perhaps where the blood runs sweet. She scratched at them until they bled. By the time she reached the marked trees, her arms were covered in bumps. She scratched and scratched until it burned. She dropped to the ground and gathered as many leaves as she possibly could and wiped her arms to relieve the burn.

The longer she went, the tired she got. The last time she followed Paul beyond the boundary wasn't quite as bad considering it was colder. The humidity wasn't helping much. She took a break by a hemlock tree and looked at her arms. They looked awful.

Swamps full of snapping turtles and frogs took over the trail, making it difficult to see where it was going. The stench of it lingered to where she could almost taste it. Crap! Lots of crap!

Then, the flies.

Ava was under attack by an horrendous raid of grain-like flies. Hundreds of them bounced off her skin, feeding as she went. Disgusted by these bugs, Ava gave her arms a good swing, hoping they'd find another victim to suck the blood from. But it was useless. The swing worked but only for a very short time. The bugs would disperse for five seconds (ten if she was lucky) before they came back.

This place is an absolute nightmare, she thought.

She followed the trail for a little bit longer, sensing the urgency that maybe she had taken a wrong turn. Muddy water broke from the swamp's border and leaked out onto the trail. The mud carried with it a rancid odor of putrid waste as it thickened like curd onto the path.

A common snapping turtle saw the whole thing from inside the swamp where his dragon yellow eyes touched the surface. His bony snout protruded from the swampy mess where his deadly jaw hooked downward.

It wasn't the snapper she was worried about. If you don't bother the snapper, the snapper won't bother you. But snakes will and it was not uncommon to stumble across a rattlesnake in these parts.

After the swamps, the bugs, and the turtles, Ava eventually found the boarding house. Chimney smoke rose from the chimney by the brook where the house slouched in its remote location. Ava managed to get close to one of the windows this time without getting caught by one of the sisters roaming the grounds.

The left corner closest by the fireplace stood three sisters, all in white, singing to the piano while the others danced cheerfully in the middle. Closest to the window was a kitchen table where George and Paul drank their waters as the girls entertained them. When the piano stopped, a violin began. It was a jamboree of sorts; a celebration.

George, having put on some weight, reclined in his chair. His belly had seen better days and bellowed out over his belt. The collared shirt lacked a few buttons but managed to stay neatly tucked inside his pants.

"They really are something," George mumbled.

He took a sip of his water, waiting patiently for Paul to respond. The girls gathered around, locking arms, and paraded in circles with the violin. When George reached his ice cubes, he settled.

"There isn't enough time for small talk," Paul said. He refused to drink the water after what he saw floating in one of the jars.

"Then you came for business I reckon."

George sat up from the chair and planted an elbow next to his empty water jar. As his simple mind wandered, the dancing went on. The years he spent living at the boarding house, built by his father in the fifties, was slow. All he desired most was a morning to kick back and listen to the violin. His father shared the same passion years before the pancreatic cancer killed him in 1969. Then, George took over the family business.

Paul watched the girls. The girl who played the violin had freckles. The one dancing alone had none. Three appeared to be too young. Another, too old. He watched some more, fishing for the perfect addition. Three girls held onto each other like monkeys in a barrel. A curly blonde was in the middle, giggling with laughter as the other two brought her around a beam.

Paul pointed, and George followed.

"Whose that?" Paul asked.

"The blonde? That's Lillian. Twenty-three in excellent condition," George said. "You won't have any trouble with that one."

"How so?"

George licked his lips and went for the jar of water, forgetting it was empty.

"I receive a lot of girls Paul on a weekly basis," George said. "Most of them have trouble with the rules but not her. Now, she's a wee bit ditzy. But aside from that, she's a prize. If I were you, I'd snatch that gem up quick before someone else does. I wouldn't be saying that either if it wasn't you Paul, so take my advice. If you have a gut feeling, then pronounce it. But, we've known each other for a long time, and I like how you think. If you take that blonde over there, I'll be generous enough to give you another."

"No, no," Paul said, shaking his head. "One is enough. I only have room for one more."

George wanted to believe what Paul was saying was true and decided to leave it at that. They shook hands and waited on the front porch while the sisters prepared Lillian for the trip. There wasn't much of a yard for viewing. Paul agreed he had a fantastic view. George, on the other hand, could care less. George sprawled his arms across the rail as Paul stood with his hands in his pockets.

"You've been married six years, haven't you?" George asked.

Paul nodded.

"You must be dedicated," George said. "Marriage is commitment. You'll never catch me wrapped up in that garbage, no offense. Living with women all my life, I could never see myself attached to one. That is not my way. No sir."

George offered Paul a cigarette from his pocket, and once Paul turned him down, George wedged the cigarette between his lips. He shielded the flickering flame from the wind and inhaled his daily intake of smoke.

Relief.

"How's your wives doing anyway?" George asked. "Haven't seen Ava or Bethany for a while now."

Paul approached the railing, taking in George's secondhand smoke.

"They're fine," Paul said.

George snickered.

"Do they know?" George asked.

"Not yet."

"No," George said. "I'm not talking about Lillian. Do they know who you *really* are?"

Paul drifted off and didn't bother to answer.

George puffed whatever was left of the cigarette before he gave the butt a good toss to the bushes.

"They're better off not knowing anyway," George said. "But truth always finds a way."

20

Burn it, a cold whispery voice told her.

Ava could sense the malevolence all around her as she stood in the cold staring at the thing that made her uncomfortable the most. Crickets chirped beneath a ghostly full moon. The forest of moonstruck trees swayed in the whirling wind. She looked at her cold feet and the match she was holding. The flame flickered in the darkness. Then, she saw the chapel. The windows weren't red anymore nor was it crawling for her flesh. It stood there in the dark, watching.

Burn it, it whispered.

The flame crawled along the shaft, allowing Ava only a short time to get rid of it before it'd scorch her fingertip. She watched the moonlight crawl across the steep roof where a True Cross erected from the sharpest point. The moon had risen to the Cross to formulate a shadow which crept its way across the ground towards Ava's direction.

The Cross crept closer in the dark.

Before the flame could reach its end, Ava tossed it towards the chapel. A wild burst of fire exploded from within, shattering the windows to an unbelievable distance. The fire grew angry as the chapel burned. The moon could no longer shine its brilliant glow once the fire reached incredible heights. Ava felt the heat radiate from the heart from where she stood. Eventually, the chapel collapsed for its walls could no longer hold against the blistering heat.

Ava thought it was beautiful as a wide grin stretched across her face. She's never been happier until she realized it was all a dream.

21

Ava wasn't thrilled about the wedding.

Lillian and Paul married on a Monday in the chapel on a sunny afternoon. The leaves had just turned from emerald green to various shades of red and yellow. The air brought a different chill when it came, forcing them to wear something heavier than what they were used to. But the wedding. Bethany was responsible for the flower arrangements by clipping her roses from the garden and putting them into lengthy glasses. Once the chapel looked respectable, Paul walked Lillian towards the decorated chapel where the marriage took place.

Bethany held the ring while Ava stood by her side, wishing what she had dreamed had come true. The pages nailed to the walls would have burned. The alter would have burned. Everything! Her eyes wandered off from the alter where Paul slipped on the silver ring, and imagined the suffering chapel engulfed in flames.

Ohhh, how I long for that moment, she thought. *The day this chapel burns to the ground will be the day I get my freedom.*

When the wedding came to a close, they spent the following months doing chores while Paul hunted. Lillian had her own bed and vanity made from the long, treacherous hours Paul spent building them. Her furniture looked better than her counterparts considering she was the new member of the family. The wood from the vanity looked higher quality and had a perfect surface. It was also darker.

Lillian brushed her hair at the vanity quite often. Ava would hide behind the other side of their bedroom door, staring at the little princess as the brush eased through each blonde strand. Envious over how beautiful Lillian was, Ava would stir the pot with Bethany in their spare time. Bethany was often shy on the subject, but a descent listener. One day when the leaves started to change, Ava took Bethany by the shoulder and spoke on the porch in private.

"That little tramp has to go," Ava told Bethany. Some of the leaves had already fallen to the ground in crispy curls. The wind would carry them off to a new place. "I can't stand living here another day with that mistake."

"What do you suggest I do about it?" Bethany asked. "Lillian isn't going anywhere."

Ava loosened her bonnet and tore it away. The white straps brushed the carpeted porch as she stood by the railing overlooking the yard. Paul was out there somewhere with his bow and arrow, waiting patiently for a deer. He wouldn't be home for another hour or so, expecting dinner when he'd walk in the room. She folded the bonnet and stood at the railing with her red hair touching her shoulders. Bethany joined her.

"Tell me more," Bethany said. "Something is on your mind."

Ava wanted to cry. She wanted to but couldn't.

"She's a little witch," Ava said, wiping away the tears. "When Paul leaves, she turns into the Devil. You should hear what she tells me sometimes. The things she says about us."

"What kind of things?" Bethany asked, demanding answers.

Ava paused to control her breathing.

"She thinks you and I are together. She jokes about how close we are. She jokes about your weight and hair. She tells me how her life isn't good enough and demands me to cover her chores for her. When Paul leaves to go hunting, she locks herself inside our bedroom for hours. Did you know that? Hours! To do what you might ask?"

Ava stopped to catch her breath.

"Don't even get me started on the brand new vanity she got," Ava said.

Bethany wrapped her arm around Ava's shoulder until Ava turned away.

"Don't do that," Ava cried.

"Do what?" Bethany asked. "What's gotten into you?"

"She's watching," Ava said. "She's always watching us. That brat will do anything spiteful to win Paul over. Don't you get it? I can't take this anymore. She has to go."

Bethany took a breath and took a seat on one of the rocking chairs. Her hands hurt from folding the cold morning laundry. They looked old and wrinkly like shriveled up raisins left out in the sun. She rocked there and listened to the chirping birds when

Ava eventually couldn't hold in her tears. She cried by the porch rail, alone.

Meanwhile, as time transpired, Lillian finished fishing for knots in her hair and came downstairs where she saw the two girls on the porch. She wiped a sticky substance from the corners of her lips and threw open the front door. Her eyes fell on Ava first before she saw Bethany in the chair.

"Well, look at this mess," Lillian said, approaching Ava.

"Leave Ava alone," Bethany shouted. She stood from the rocking chair with her fists in a ball.

"And what are you going to do about it, sleazeball?" Lillian asked. She stood firmly on the porch in her favorite sapphire blue dress accompanied by a pair of shined shoes. Her hazel eyes seemed to burn a hole into Bethany's when she'd stare. With the end of every sentence, Lillian sparked an attitude that would kick a camel on the rump.

Bethany didn't buy into Lillian's intimidation business. Instead, she looked into Lillian's eyes and smirked. At first, Lillian backed away before she took in Bethany's serious threat.

"I want you to take a good look at Ava," Bethany said. "If I ever see Ava like this again because of your wrong doing, I will strangle you. Rules or no rules, I will make your suffering so slow and agonizing, you'd wish you'd kept your trap shut."

"Is that suppose to scare me?" Lillian whispered. She stepped closer to Bethany with stupidity sunken into her eyes.

Come closer, Bethany thought. *That's it...*

"Paul comes home in an hour," Lillian said. "And if he finds out that you two haven't been keeping up with your chores, you'll come crying to me. And you know where I'll be when that happens? I'll be sitting on the staircase clapping away with a wide grin on my face because the look in your crying eyes will keep me happy for a long time."

Lillian's eyes went to Ava, slumped against the railing in sorrow.

"I hope he gets to you first," Lillian said.

Ava looked at Lillian in terror.

"I hope he rips right into you, blouse and all," Lillian said, smirking. A sunken dimple outside Lillian's right laugh line was the last thing Ava saw before she buried her weeping face into the hollow of her crossed arms. There, Ava's back rose slightly after each sob.

Lillian came back to Bethany again.

"I cannot tell you how impatient I am for when that day comes," Lillian promised. "Do you want to know why?"

Bethany said nothing.

"Because I will always be his perfect sweetheart," she whispered. "As for you? You will always be an embarrassment."

22

Winter.

It was the third of December when a fierce blizzard, among one of the worst Paul had seen in a very long time, decided to dump five feet of snow on the region. The storm worsened by the third day, practically caving Paul and his three wives inside for the night. While the girls prepared dinner in the kitchen, Paul had his hands baking by the fire. Powerful gusts of snow slammed against the outer wall, disrupting the buck head Paul shot three weeks prior to the storm. The whirls of wind sounded like a war causing all of them to shutter. Canons sounded from the west from pines collapsing due to the weight of the snow. Three collapses occurred while the girls rounded up the plates after a warming meal. The fourth sent a disturbance throughout the cabin, causing Paul to open the curtain into a world of cold darkness.

"Will we be alright here?" Bethany asked. She stood by the fireplace with the poker in her hand. The fire crackled by her side, sending a cloud of fireflies up the stone chimney.

Paul closed the curtain after realizing he couldn't see behind the slate of glass. He returned to his chair where the air was warm and held up his hands again.

"Just another pine falling from the wind," he said. "We will be fine."

Bethany collected the dishes as Ava dried them. Lillian simply watched from the cold box where they kept the deer meat stored. When the winds started to rattle the windows, that's when all of them joined Paul by the fire. The aroma of burning wood filled the interior as well as its godly flame. Paul decided it was time to throw another log onto the steaming grill where embers slept in their charcoal grave. Ava made her rounds by striking five matches and lighting candles to give the hidden spots where the fire couldn't seem to reach some life. When she finished, she returned to the fire where Bethany sat alone. Paul and Lillian joined hands on the other side of the cabin, dancing swiftly to Enya's *Caribbean Blue*.

"Who ever thought he'd get married for the third time," Bethany whispered to Ava, watching the two mingle in the air to Enya's beautiful voice. "He even gave Lillian her own record for personal use. You would never catch him giving us anything like that. Only fabric to sow our own dresses and skirts."

Ava didn't seem to mind the music. She found Enya's voice so relaxing as if humanity actually possessed a slice of Heaven. She watched the flames flicker again, unleashing a second dose of fireflies up the chimney. The dancing embers took her mind elsewhere as the record player played Enya's *Orinoco Flow*.

"You were right Ava," Bethany said. "She's a real troublemaker. I caught her drifting off the trails again after she found you going to the island in the stream. Apparently, she's been watching you like a hawk so I'd grow eyes in the back of your head if I were you."

"Has she crossed the boundary?"

"Who knows what she's capable of doing?" Bethany said. "Are you still crossing it?"

Ava faced the fire's heat, trying desperately to avoid the question at all cost.

"Ava?" Bethany whispered. "Did you do it?"

"Maybe..."

"Ava! You promised!" Bethany said.

"I wanted to see it for myself."

Bethany grunted softly to herself when she saw Lillian's chin propped on Paul's shoulder as they slow danced to Enya's final song *Only Time*. Their dance felt true and romantic at heart. Paul looked truly happy as if the search was finally over. He found what he was after--someone who understood his ways. Paul broke his concentration from the floor and wiggled his nose to hers. Her head fell back in laughter as he guided her back to the floor before lifting her up again.

"Are you mad at me?" Ava asked.

Bethany took one look at Ava and shook her head.

"Do you think they're in love?" Bethany said, watching the pair finish their dance.

Before Ava had the chance to answer, their warm evening suddenly went cold when the front door violently came open. Lillian screamed as gusts of cold snow flooded the room. Paul left her side and ran for the door. But to his dismay, the snow on the floor was the least of his worries. The only thought on his fuzzy mind was what had opened the door in the first place, and it wasn't the snow. It was a man wearing a bear coat and raccoon hat. The man was on his hands and knees, shivering from the cold. He made these weird wheezing sounds when Paul came to the man's rescue.

"Holy crows!" the bearded man shouted. "Colder than an ice chest out there."

"Ava," Paul shouted. "Get this man some warm towels."

As Ava obeyed his commands, Paul had the man on his feet. He was taller than Paul, almost coming in around six feet tall. When he crossed his arms to shield away from the blistering cold, he looked like a bear himself. The brown eyes in his sockets examined the warm cabin with much delight.

"Pardon the intrusion," the man said. "But that cold is for the birds. Good Lord almighty."

Ava brought the warm towels soaked in warm water and brought the man to the fire. Ava and Bethany took the liberty in removing the bear coat as well as the man's under garments. They dug layer after layer until they reached a bare chest full of swirly hair.

"Much obliged ladies," the man said, chuckling. "Service at its finest."

Bethany threw the towel over the man's chest before removing his boots. Ava offered him a cup of nice hot cocoa in which was accepted with gratitude. Ava fixed a cushion behind his hairy neck as he sipped at the warm substance, licking his lips in pleasure.

Lillian followed Paul to the fireplace where everyone seemed attracted. When the man finished his cocoa with great satisfaction, he held up his trembling hands to the fire while his snowy clothes dripped at the mantel.

"So," Paul started. He held Lillian's hand who had her legs crossed. "Where are you from, and what brings you here in the middle of a wicked blizzard?"

"Ah," the man said, chuckling. The crow's feet outside his eyes thickened when he was struck with a thought. He sat up in his chair and brought his hands together. The towel felt lukewarm at the touch when Ava came from behind to check on it. "My name is Shawn and I come from the North. Erie, Pennsylvania to be exact."

Bethany found his brown eyes to be mysterious as they traveled the cabin's interior. He fancied cabin's architecture, very pleased on the hardship of where the logs came together to form the wall. He took everything in all at once.

"It's funny," Shawn said, staring off into the hot embers. "A few days ago I was hunting deer unaware of the snowstorm coming my way. How foolish of me."

Shawn took one of his drenched socks off to find a foot swollen with frostbite. He cringed at the sight of it, almost ill to the stomach.

"Would you look at that," Shawn said. He didn't seem bothered by the frostbite on an emotional level as he was on the physical. He attempted to wiggle his toes, trying to find out if there was any movement at all. Unfortunately for poor Shawn, his toes were frozen in time. "Well, ain't that a pity."

They all looked at the skin condition with disgust. Three of five toes were swollen to the point they were pressed tightly together as a blistering red inflammation discolored each toe. Two of his fingers had started the process but nothing too concerning. But nothing about Shawn's condition required surgical removal of his toes or finger but if he had served anymore of his time outside in the cold, he would have.

"Is there anything else we can get you Shawn?" Paul asked.

"No sir," Shawn said, grinning. "Again, I cannot thank you guys enough for helping me. Without you, your wife, and kids, I would have died in that blizzard."

"My name is Paul, and I have no children. This is Lillian. Over there is Ava and Bethany. I'm married to all three."

It didn't take long for Shawn's cheeks to turn cherry red.

"Pardon me," he said. "I had no idea. You have no idea how lucky you are Paul. Such beautiful wives you've got here. Man!" He slapped his inner thigh with his frostbitten hand and chuckled.

"Thank you," Paul said. He laughed himself before Lillian joined in. Ava and Bethany stared from the couch.

"Well," Paul said. "Considering this storm is not going to lighten up anytime soon, you are welcome to stay until it passes. You have access to our food and water. Bethany shall fix the couch with some spare covers we keep upstairs. Ava, you can make our guest a turkey sandwich. I'm sure you're probably starving from all that hard work in the snow."

"Famished," Shawn said. When he smiled, his whole face seemed to vanish beneath his jolly wrinkles. Bethany pictured him as a heavy-set St. Nicholas. "I want to thank you again Paul for bringing me in. Such a privilege."

After Shawn ate his sandwich, told his jokes, and made them all laugh, Bethany fixed a place for Shawn to spend the night. She folded a thin quilt in half, placed it on the cushions, and threw another quilt over a pillow. Paul retired for the night with Lillian considering it was her turn to share the covers. Bethany changed to her night gown while Ava stoked the fire. Shawn was already under the covers with his head faced towards the fireplace. He watched Ava as she'd bend her rump forward, keeping his naughty thoughts to himself.

"You've been married long?" Shawn asked. "Paul comes off as a nice character. A little on the strict side but still half descent."

Ava crept to one of the rocking chairs and sat down. Her back ached from all the excitement.

"You're clothes should be dry by dawn," she said. "Your boots will take the longest time to dry but as soon as the sun rises, I'll put them close to an optimal flame. Is there anything else I can do for you, Shawn?"

"You're a pretty little thing," he said. "You know that right?"

He smiled again.

"You should get some rest," she said, ignoring the question. "The night is upon us."

"So it is," Shawn said, ducking under the covers. "So it is."

23

The blizzard went on for another three days and two nights since Shawn's unexpected arrival. The men worked on clearing a pathway from the cabin to the chapel where Paul spent fifteen minutes explaining their way-of-life to Shawn. Ava watched them from inside, wondering what lies Paul was feeding Shawn. What kind of picture was he really painting?

Bethany swept a pile of dust into the scoop in the kitchen and disposed of it. Her chores were concentrated on getting most of the floor swept and the wood polished. Lillian spent her hours upstairs folding laundry, cleaning the tub, and wiping the windows. Ava closed the curtain and went to the kitchen.

"Have they reached the chapel yet?" Bethany asked. "I saw you standing by the window monitoring their progress."

Ava sensed the irritation in her voice as she leaned against the ice box. Bethany propped the broom against the West wall and flattened out her white apron. Her next destination would be the counter where she would dice some granny apples.

"You're still mad at me about the promise I made several months ago?"

Bethany reached for the kitchen knife and started slicing. Each slice carried a solid knock sound from the cutting board.

"I'm just disappointed in you Ava," Bethany said. "If you make a promise, you keep it. You could have gotten us in a lot of trouble if Paul found out. The boundary isn't meant to be crossed for a reason. You know this."

"It's to keep us in," Ava said. "I know, but isn't that the problem? You've never wondered what the real world is like? The one you were stolen from all because we were born inside a stupid family cult? This may be our chance, Bethany."

Bethany slammed the knife against the block and paused.

"Our chance to do what?" she asked. "What part of this hasn't sunk in yet? We are stuck here. We have no where to go. Why don't you accept it and move on. Just move on Bethany."

Bethany untied her apron and threw it across the counter in tears. Ava wished she had apologized, but Bethany had already climbed the stairs before she had an opportunity to do so. Instead, Ava finished the apples. Then, she returned by the window and opened the curtain. The men spoke amongst themselves while hoisting large amounts of snow from the chapel door. When they finished, Paul opened the chapel for Shawn.

Instead of lighting the downstairs with the fireplace, Paul worked on the wood stove instead. Shawn joined him by making sure they had enough wood for the night while Ava prepared dinner. Life in the winter season was long and boring. And nobody really cared for it except for Lillian. Ava and Bethany endured their long hours with Paul in the house since the snow drift deterred him from leaving. But Shawn was present to keep Paul company which Ava viewed as a blessing in disguise. At least, it kept Paul from being picky about the chores being done.

The table was set and the dinner prepared. They had deer steaks, potatoes, and blueberries by candlelight. Ava picked at her potatoes while she watched the others eat their steaks. The sight of them chomping down on their blood-soaked meat like a pack of hungry wolves repulsed her. And as the evening went on like this, Ava kept her eyes on her potatoes.

"What a delicious dinner," Shawn said, licking his fingers. "Is this deer meat?"

Paul nodded as the meat struggled under the knife. When the blade eventually went through, it scraped the plate underneath. Blood settled like brown broth on the plate.

"Your hospitality continues to impress me," Shawn said.

As soon as Ava lifted her eyes from her plate and saw the blood oozing from Shawn's lips, she stood up from the table and ran upstairs to the bathroom. The exhaustion from puking up liquid set her back for a few minutes. She wiped the sweat from her brow and lifted her dress. Her belly had shrunken even worse so, exposing a line of ribs. Tears filled her eyes as she lowered the dress. She wept by the sink basin while the dinner continued without her.

As picky as Paul was with his gear being in the right place at all times, Ava noticed he had left a pair of grooming scissors on the sink. She reached for them, intrigued by the sharpness of each blade. Sharp enough for deep incisions. By holding the scissors upright in the candlelight, she ran her fingertip along the edge in order to grasp the reality of damage this instrument could cause.

One cut is all it would take, she thought. Everything seemed clear now. From what she could see by sitting on the floor, there was no other option. Nobody would miss her, and nobody would care. It would be her choice alone; not Paul's.

She snapped the blades shut and reopened them.

Snap.

They were heavy to the touch and cold. *This is real*, she thought. *I'm holding something small enough to make an substantial difference.* First, the numbness. Then, the pain. But not as painful as what she was feeling. No, this would make it all disappear.

How would she do it?

Ava pulled a clump of hair away from her neck and held the blade beneath her chin. The neck seemed like a descent spot. What a terrible mess it'd make for Bethany. No, we cannot have that. She brought the blade to her naked wrist. Here, maybe? The cut would be an obvious way to end things for certain but she feared it wouldn't be quick enough. And the mess it would make! What a terrible way to go having to dump a gruesome mess on Bethany's behalf.

She looked at the blade. Then, her shaky wrist. The veins looked nice and thick, pumped full of blood. Just one cut looked enticing. She rested the blade horizontally against her wrist and waited patiently for her adrenaline to kick in. She wanted to do it so bad. *Just get it out of the way!* she thought. *It will all be over soon. Just a quick cut is all it takes. Then, lights out Alice.*

Tears again. They never stop. She bit her lip, looked at the blade on her wrist, and decided it wasn't worth it. Her hands fell lifelessly beside her as she took a breath of relief. The scissors slid across the floor. Any further, she would have spent the next fifteen minutes searching for them beneath the tub. Ava bundled herself up into a secure ball against the wall and cried again.

So close, she thought. *But not close enough.*

After her little episode with the scissors, she dipped her face into the sink basin, and decided it was time to put the scissors where they belong. Instead of inside her wrist, Ava placed them inside Paul's bathroom bag by the closet where the towels were stored. When she rejoined them downstairs, they had already finished their dinner. Shawn was telling stories by an empty fireplace while the rest of them stared in awe. Ava found her seat on the couch next to Bethany who yawned for the fourth time that evening. Paul and Lillian were glued to the other couch where they were hypnotized by Shawn who sounded like he owned the place. Both feet were still frostbitten.

"And that's how I got involved in big game," Shawn said, finishing his story.

"What a history," Paul said. He kissed Lillian's hand and grinned. "Tell us about your family."

"No," he said, cheerfully. He took a sip of his water and brushed his beard. "No family."

"No wife either?" Lillian asked.

"No little misses," Shawn replied. There was a twinkle in his eye. "No wife. Never really seemed to have an interest settling down. I'm gone far too much to settle anywhere really. I used to call Erie my home until I moved down here in Clearfield County. Work at the mill got fuzzy. Hunting wasn't all that great. So, I started working at that factory over there about ten miles West of here."

"I know the place," Paul said. "They've had a rough year haven't they? The last I've heard about the factory was their hiring freeze."

Shawn took another sip before he finished the glass.

"I came after the place froze over. The hiring benefit issues turned the managers all into gremlins. They're a bunch of horse apples. But enough about me," Shawn said. "Tell me a little about yourself? What do you do?"

The girls all looked at Paul as if the Jack had finally found his way out of his box.

"We are simpletons on this neck of the woods," Paul said. "We do things differently here than people do on the outside. In a way, our sheltered life serves us protection from all the nastiness in the world."

"And there's nothing wrong with that," Shawn said. "You have yourself three beautiful young wives, a clean house, and a little church in the yard. Nothing can beat having a life such as yours."

Paul cleared his throat.

"It's a chapel Shawn," Paul said. "Not a church. I thank you for the compliment."

Shawn went for his glass not realizing until later he had already emptied it. Lillian, who had locked eyes on Shawn throughout the whole evening, stood up to Shawn's calling and took the glass.

"I'll fill this up for you," Lillian said, walking the glass to the kitchen.

"Well then," Paul said. He stood up beside Shawn. "While Lillian does that, I'd like to show you my records. Ava and Bethany, you girls take care of the wood stove and make sure there's enough wood in there so we don't turn to frozen mummies over the course of the night."

While Paul and Shawn climbed the stairs discussing the eighties, Lillian followed with a glass full of water and ice cubes. Ava and Bethany met by the wood stove. Ava threw another two logs into the stove's opon mouth while Bethany leaned against the wood pile.

"Have you been watching Lillian lately?" Bethany asked. "She has the hots for Shawn. Can't stop staring at him for one second."

Ava closed the lid and faced Bethany.

"I haven't been watching," Ava said, thinking about the episode that transpired in the upstairs bathroom. It was an episode Ava would end up taking to the grave. "Does Paul know that she's been staring at Shawn?"

Bethany shook her head as she chewed the inner lining of her cheek.

"I don't think so," she said. "But Paul's so far up Shawn's crack he probably has to take a second to figure out where he is when he comes back to reality. But Lillian." Bethany shook her head with amazement. "She's stuck to Shawn like putty."

"I wish she disappears," Ava said. "Just curls up and vanishes in the wind."

"Things don't happen that way."

"We'll see," Ava said, acting as though she knew something Bethany didn't. "Lillian sticks to patterns. And she isn't the smartest cookie. I can see her messing up. I truly can. And when that day comes, I'll be the one laughing, not her."

It turned out Ava was right all along when Shawn went to bed. Bethany had some sense that it would only be a matter of time before Lillian would betray Paul. A feeling of misfortune overcame Bethany as soon as she closed her eyes. Sweet dreams never came. Instead, she thought about what Ava had told her by the wood stove. She prayed it wouldn't happen. But sometimes, even prayers don't get answered in the form we want them to.

24

Deception would have be betrayal's ugly cousin. Indeed, if deception sprouted arms and legs one day, he would be beautiful on the outside. But inside, he'd have the heart of a rattlesnake. Ava couldn't imagine how enticing it was for Eve to accept the forbidden fruit offered by a cunning serpent in the Garden of Eden. For all of humanity to suffer by the fingertips of just one woman, the fruit had to have been so appealing to the eye even the first woman to walk the earth had no option but to take it. Not only did the deceptive snake fool one child of God, it fooled two with the same fruit. Two birds died with one stone that day, and it only takes one rotten apple to spoil the bunch.

It was the same night Ava debated on suicide when she woke up from another one of her vivid dreams. The dream had yet to provide answers or some kind of clue on whether or not it was a premonition. The chapel still burned in her mind, an act she herself couldn't even picture herself doing even though she found pleasure by breaking the rules. There must have been something she missed, something with great meaning. Bethany would have called it faith. Ava considered it fate.

Eager for an ice cold glass of water, Ava struck a match to light the candle by her bedside, and slowly descended the stairs. The candlelight danced along the walls as she peeled away the darkness. Each step seemed to last forever like a stairway descending into the depths of Hell, not even realizing that was indeed where she'd end up in just a few more seconds.

Step after step. When the flame exposed the last stair, Ava made her turn around the railing, struck by what she saw. An intense burst of terror ravished her by the railing as if the sight of Medusa had turned her into stone. All her thoughts were seized. Nothing came in; nothing came out. She couldn't breathe. She couldn't talk. All of her bodily functions she learned to love so much stopped working. Air felt like a thick razor blade traveling down the dark tunnel of her throat. When she decided to steer the candlelight even further into the shadows, it all came to an end.

What did Ava see exactly?

It was Shawn, lying on his back as he motioned Lillian on top of his hairy chest. Their naked bodies swam within the sweaty sheets and quilt as they communicated in their once-secretive darkness. Now, they were caught in the act. Ava would have no choice but to blow the whistle on her fellow sister and their uninvited guest. But as soon as Ava regained feeling in her legs, she saw something else lurking in the nearby corner. She turned her head slowly, keeping the candlelight as still as possible.

Then, it happened.

What Ava had seen in the gloomy corner was the tip of an arrow point. Three razor sharp edges were aimed at its designated target. Once Ava caught sight of the point, it was already well on its way towards the couch where it pierced Lillian three inches beneath her collarbone. The instant hit caused Lillian's body to stop the motion in a dead standstill as her brain tried to ponder over what events had just materialized. The only thing that moved on Lillian other than her naked breasts were her flickering eyes. Then, her entire body fell limp.

As soon as Shawn awoke from his dreamlike state and saw the arrow protruding out of Lillian's bleeding chest, it was already too late. A second arrow stung the air between its new target and the hunter. The point swiveled freely in the darkness for a split second before it demolished Shawn's brains. He died instantly with his hands still wrapped around Lillian's warm waist.

Ava screamed when she dropped the candle to the floor. A boot trampled on the flame before it had anytime to catch. Then, Ava was pushed back against the North wall that kept the wood stove separate from the living room. A massive hand cupped her mouth hard enough to seal out anything trying to get in. She breathed through her nose as two eyes of fluorescent blue entered the fragmented moonlight. Everything else remained hidden.

"*Shhh*," Paul whispered. "The eyes can easily deceive us but the heart knows. I have two arrows left and they're already locked in. I'm going to give you one chance to answer my question truthfully. If there are any flaws to your story, I will end you just as I've ended them. Blink once if you understand."

Ava blinked.

"Did you or did you not have sexual interaction with Shawn? Blink once if you did."

Ava blinked twice rather quickly.

"One more question," Paul said, cupping her lips harder. "Did Bethany have sexual interaction with Shawn? Same deal as before, blink once if she did to your knowledge."

Ava blinked twice again, rather quickly.

"I'm going to let go now," Paul said. "Bethany will be joining us at any moment. Promise me you will calm her down when she sees what had happened. Blink only once."

Ava blinked.

"That's a good girl," he said, grinning.

Paul loosened his grip before he disappeared into the darkness. Ava was left behind as she slowly regained feeling in her lips. It wasn't long before Paul had several candles lit. The murder scene came alive, and that's when Ava heard Bethany's footsteps thumping down the staircase.

Not long after that, Bethany screamed.

25

Snow drift continued on for hours the night of Shawn and Lillian's death. Bethany and Ava watched Paul wrap the bodies in blankets as the wind rattled the walls. Bethany reached for Ava's hand and held it tight as they watched.

Once the bodies were wrapped and tied with rope, Paul drug them to the open door where snow had drifted in. A trail of dark blood was left behind as he piled one over the other. Paul broke into a sweat when he reached for his handkerchief. He gave his forehead a swift wipe before it disappeared into his back pocket. Then, he went at it again.

"I still don't understand why you had to kill them," Bethany said. Her voice was all shook up. "Couldn't you've just punished her like any other time? Why did she have to go like that?"

Paul rose from the body and stared at Bethany. It wasn't long before his forehead was covered in sweat again. This time, wiping the sweat away slipped his mind.

"Lillian was filled with evil," Paul said. "They both were. It's better this way. And besides, Lillian knew the penalty for betraying our marriage. She could have have made a different decision. But this is what she chose."

All three of them looked at the dead bodies by the door.

"You may think this is a game," he said. "Look at them. This is what happens when you disobey the rules. You break them, you get punished. Ava, help me with Shawn's legs. We will carry them both to the porch until morning. Then, I'll choose respectful burial."

Ava did what Paul asked and grabbed Shawn's legs. The body felt heavy as they walked it outside to the porch where snow had drifted several feet from the screen. They followed the same procedure for Lillian's body only hers wasn't quite as hard to move as Shawn's was. Ava made sure the covers were tight so nothing could expose itself in the fierce winds. Then, she followed Paul inside where he lit a fire. Bethany still preached the wrongdoing of Paul's actions, even if death was what they deserved. She didn't think it was right for Paul to just end their lives like that. And if that was easy, what was he capable of doing to them if one of his buttons got pushed too far over the edge?

The fire popped as soon as Paul introduced it with more fuel. He poked it several times with the poker before he finally left it crackle for a while. He remained by the stone bench by the fire as the girls sat on the couch beside each other. The cabin went cold and it would have taken hours for the fire to heat the upstairs completely. They would have no choice but to spend the night downstairs where the murder took place.

"Nobody will notice," Paul said. He rubbed his blood-stained fingers together. "We will bury the evidence by the chapel tomorrow. Both of you will ignore the chores tomorrow and tend to the blood trail. It's important that we take good care of this before the snow melts. I'm sure people will come looking for Shawn so we must pay close attention to the details."

"What will we say?" Ava asked.

"You will tell the authorities you haven't heard anything," he said. "They'll probably want to search the place. Let them. Pay no attention to the specific questions they'll ask of you. Be as general as you can like you've never met the guy. Pretend he never even stumbled in that night. I'll take care of the rest."

"And Lillian?" Bethany asked. "What about her?"

Paul shook his head.

"Nobody knows she exists," he said. "No one will come looking for her. You'll clean the floors with hot water. Once that dries, you'll cover the boards with a fresh layer of polish. We need to make sure all the blood is tended to before it settles into the cracks. I'll see about maybe getting fresh paint in the next few days. Maybe we could hide it with that but until then, we wash and polish."

They stayed by the fire for a while until they decided it was time to call it a night. All three of them avoided sleeping by the blood trail or the couch considering that's where the crime took place. Bethany had thrown a cover in front of the fireplace. Paul removed his shirt as the girls took off their gowns.

At last, they slept.

26

The snow crumbled beneath their boots when they reached the stream. The water chiseled its way through the wintery wonderland, forming icicles along the bank. It was cold enough for hyperthermia if one would happen to accidentally fall in. Ava knelt beside the opening to the stream and dipped her finger in. The cold ate through the finger and chilled the bone. She pulled it out and glanced at the waterfall. Ice dangled from the rocks as the water roared down the cliff. The train tracks on a distant bridge behind the waterfall was nothing but a snow wall. Whatever had grown there died months ago.

Bethany pressed her coat tight against her neck, hoping to seal off any sign of opening for the cold to creep in. She stood behind Ava, watching the water as it'd fall from the ice. Paul stayed at the cabin, digging holes for the burial while Ava agreed to fetch some buckets of water. Bethany had followed her but it wasn't for the water. She approached Ava's side and reached for her cold hand.

"You're scared, aren't you?" Ava asked. As the breath exited her mouth, a cloud of smoke formed. She was indeed cold, very cold. Not enough clothes could shield her from the wind, snow, and ice. She clenched Bethany's hand and focused on the water swirling five feet ahead of them.

"I want out Ava," Bethany said. "I can't bare to spend another night at that cabin anymore. He's turned bad. Ever since he brought Lillian home, he's changed somehow."

Ava closed her eyes and listened. The water acted as white noise working against the chaos that had formed in the past six years of her life. Somehow, the stream was always there for her. Maybe, there was a God. She turned away from the water and held Bethany, assuming that perhaps she was right all along. Somewhere out there, someone was calling her name. It explained the vivid dreams she had, the voices, and the series of strange events.

"I want you to listen to me," Ava said. She paused for a moment in order for her mind to collect her thoughts. The chill from the water started to freeze her words before she could actually get them out into the open. "I'm planning an escape."

"B-but how?" Bethany stuttered. She shook while Ava turned towards the water again.

"Through there," Ava said, pointing towards the island. But beyond the island there existed a place Ava had visited before. Crossing the island was forbidden of course, which concerned Bethany. She wondered if Ava had it in her. "If we cross the stream, we will walk through the woods for about two miles before we come across a pond. I've been there before. Once we reach the pond, we should be distant enough to keep going without having to worry about Paul. Knowing him, he won't have a clue on which way to go afterwards. The pond is our only chance. If both of us aren't up to the challenge, then it's useless."

Bundled like an Eskimo, Bethany grew curious about crossing the boundary. Freedom sounded sweet to her cloudy mind which hasn't seen the real world in five years. Escaping sounded like a swell plan, but it posed a risk.

"What if Paul catches up to us before we would reach the pond?"

Ava didn't want to say it, but she did.

"I'm afraid he'd kill us both," she said. She looked at the line of snowy trees across the stream and pictured it like it was in the summer. "I'm only thinking logically here. Based on what we've seen last night, he's capable of spilling blood. We both know that for certain now. If you're ready to follow through with it, I'll stand by you all the way. But if we agree to do this, we will leave tomorrow morning. Paul sleeps in longer during the winter. That will give us a steady head start before he sniffs us out."

"That's what I'm afraid of," Bethany said.

Ava scooped three buckets worth of water before they walked the trail back home, pondering over their plan of escape. Thrilled by the idea, Ava couldn't let it leave her mind. It was something they should have executed a long time ago, way before Lillian was ever introduced. But Bethany felt skeptical; not so easily convinced by Ava's plans.

The summer months have passed which meant they had the snow to worry about. Snow meant footprints which were easy to follow especially for a seasoned hunter. Even if Ava came close to accuracy in regards to the scenario she pitched at the stream, the pond wouldn't save them. Paul would follow their tracks clear until they were too tired to walk anymore. He'd kill them for sure.

Ava stopped by a clump of white boulders and relaxed the tension from her aching shoulders.

"It's now or never," Ava said. "What will it be? You and I must be willing to follow through because we can work together."

"I'm not sure about this Ava," she said. "It sounds risky."

"I need a decision now," Ava said. "We won't be able to leave the cabin for several days so now is our chance to collaborate on this. Please give me something."

Bethany had no choice but to give the go ahead.

"Okay," Bethany said, nodding. "There have been times in my life where I wasn't sure about something, but this I am. I want to leave Ava, and I want to experience the world with you. Just you and I."

"Good," Ava said, lifting the heavy buckets. "We leave at dawn."

27

Escaping polygamy found its structure in a week long curriculum taught at George's boarding house by the lead sisters. The task meant to frighten the youths as much as possible to prevent anyone from damaging its reputation as a structured group. Even George had amended its design, hoping no woman would ever defeat its purpose. And if had, exile would be fit for the deviant.

Ava and Bethany could have cared less about exile. Hundreds of women before them had gone through the same levels of mental exhaustion and none of them have ever escaped. Too many feared the rules which acted as stakes in an open relationship. These stakes were meant to keep wives from wandering off beyond the boundaries where a new world awaited them. Ava felt powerful and unstoppable now that she had Bethany on her side. They would fight for their everlasting freedom even if it took all they had to defeat the dragon. The fight wouldn't come easy. Paul spent many years training for a messy upbringing. A mentally charged male whose wives were planning to abandon his way of life proved to be a recipe for disaster. But they weren't turning back. It was too late for that now.

The floorboards were washed and polished. Bethany spent hours on the floors before she decided to dust the mantel, the dining room set, and the counters. Everything appeared to shine. Upstairs, Ava worked on each individual room. She finished at Paul's bedroom where she found the Holy Bible lying on the face of one of his desks. She tucked the smelly rag into the pocket of her white apron and opened the book.

Her fingers flipped through the pages, her eyes mesmerized by all of the notes Paul had tucked in the spine. But something caught her eye. By the time she reached the middle of the book, a thick piece of card stock fell to the floor. She reached for it and read it silently.

Bethany had just got done organizing the chunks of wood by the fireplace when she heard Ava running down the stairs in a whirlpool of sadness. Tears rolled down her cheeks when she approached Bethany, handing over the piece of card stock into her possession.

"That fool has been lying to us the whole time," Ava cried. "I cannot believe this is happening!"

A sickness began to claw away at the inner lining of Bethany's stomach when she opened the note and slowly began to read it.

"Where did you find this?" Bethany asked.

Ava was too upset to answer. She threw her hands over her head and wailed.

"Ava," she said. "Answer me. Where did you find this note?"

"Upstairs," Ava cried. "In Paul's Bible."

Ava shot towards the couch and quickly unraveled her emotions. Six years of pain finally rushed to the surface, something she had been storing for a long time. Bethany felt heartbroken but insensitive at the same time.

"So you're telling me you didn't know about this?" Bethany asked. "He's never told you?"

Ava looked at Bethany in shock.

"You knew?" Ava asked.

"Of course I knew," she said. "I was under the impression that you've known all along."

"How long have you known about this?" Ava cried. Never-ending tears suddenly streamed from her eyes as if a levee had broken.

"He told me," she said. "Five years ago."

"*How...*" Ava whispered, her voice barely unrecognizable. She closed her eyes and thrashed her chest forward as her hands transformed to claws. She hated the world and everyone in it.

Burn it! she thought. *Burn this house, this chapel, this life! Burn it all to ashes!*

"I'm sorry Ava," Bethany said. "I really had no idea."

Bethany glanced at the note once more before she crumbled it between her fingers. It was in George's handwriting: *I give this Bible as a gift for partnering up with your dear, loving niece. You two will make a fine looking couple. Love, -G.*

It was an entrapment of a horrible marriage. Bethany comforted Ava while she finished crying. The note meant nothing to Bethany as it did to Ava. She couldn't imagine how Paul had kept it a secret for all those years. Perhaps, he was a coward after all. A yellow-bellied coward. Ava wiped the tears away and faced the window. Snow fell from the sky in small numbers, not enough to accumulate.

"He's never told me Bethany," Ava said. "He's kept the truth hidden from me for all these years. How could he have done that?"

Bethany brought Ava's head to her breast and stroked her hair.

"You were never meant to find out, I suppose. But unfortunately, you did. Now you see the truth behind Paul and this religion. It's all fake, Ava. We've been living a fake life for years. But it wasn't wasted."

"How can you say that?" Ava said, raising her head. "How is my life here not wasted? He stole it."

"You and I would have never met," Bethany replied.

"And I suppose you have no relation to him?" Ava asked. "You're an outsider?"

"I share no relation," she answered. "Only through marriage. I understand he has hurt us. He may be our husband and your uncle, but we still need to forgive him. Don't let hate swallow you, Ava."

"He's been inside me!" Ava shouted. "How can I forgive that!"

"Do try, Ava."

Paul finished burying the bodies late that afternoon. Snow flakes had collected on his broad shoulders when he opened the porch door to slide in the dirty shovel. He watched the snowfall for a little while. As he sat there, he thought about the next step. One day, the authorities would come looking for Shawn. Then, the questions. He would deny everything, of course, but his two wives concerned him.

What if they screw this up? he thought. They'll search the house to make sure. That was for certain. By that point, hopefully Bethany could plant more roses around the chapel in order to disguise the burial site. Eventually, the rose bushes would grow over the disturbed ground keeping the bodies a secret forever. Still, he had another four months to go before he'd be in the clear. He looked at the graves beside the chapel. Two mounds of snow and mud was all the evidence they would need to make a conviction.

Now, he was in trouble. Big trouble.

The front door opened, scaring Ava half to death. Paul stepped in from the cold and slammed the door shut before checking the lock. He hung his jacket on the coat tree before making his way towards the fireplace. Slapping his rough hands together, he looked out the window. The graves were obvious. Too obvious.

"We need a new plan," Paul said. "The graves are too shallow and they look too obvious to fool any officer. We will have to wait it out someplace else until the snow begins to melt. That way, the ground will be soft enough for deeper graves."

"But where would we go?" Bethany asked. "The boarding house is-"

Bethany stopped herself but it was too late. Ava closed her eyes and brought her hand to her face as if to block out the disaster ready to happen. Paul's hands broke apart and met his side when he walked slowly towards Bethany. Ava could see the evil in this man's eyes. Normally a flare would take some building before the hell storm would start. But not this time. He had all the information he needed.

"What did you say?" he asked.

His jaw tightened which defined some strong cheekbones. His brows bowed when his eyes glared. One hand dug into the fine leather as the other made its way towards Bethany's throat. Ava learned to predict Paul's flares. First, the intimidation factor. Then, the questions. Then finally, the pain.

Bethany panicked. Her mind started to spin out of control as she tried to think of something to make it all better. But nothing came. Paul got closer until she could feel his warm breath in her face. The smell of his sweaty body odor lingered like a rotten block of cheese.

"I didn't say anything," she said.

"You said boarding house," he said. "For you to know where the boarding house is, you've had to cross the boundary. Did you cross it?"

Bethany yelped like a dog when he snatched a clump of her hair between his fingers and yanked. Some of the loose strands snapped from her scalp but this didn't stop him. He pulled harder until she couldn't deal with the pain anymore.

"Yes," she said, finally. "I crossed the boundary."

The real pain began when her words sunk in. Paul loosened his grip, cupped his strong hand behind Bethany's neck, and hoisted her body from the couch and onto the floor. Bethany took out two wooden chairs and a wood chipping of floorboard, breaking her left leg in the process. Tears streamed from her face when the numbing faded. Reaching for the lifeless limb, she cried in horror as Paul towered over her.

The flesh surrounding her kneecap swelled and bruised. Attempting to walk would be useless considering everything below her pelvis felt dead. Paul stood over her torso with his massive body with his hands spread apart like claws and mouth wide open in anger.

"What have I told you girls about crossing the boundary!" he shouted.

He lifted one leg and brought it down on Bethany's knee, shattering it for the second time. The sounds of cracking bones stung their ears as Bethany's cries grew louder. By the sight of the shattered kneecap, she feared she wouldn't be able to walk anymore. But Bethany refused to give up. She used up all the energy she had left in her towards Paul by swatting, slapping, and hitting. Nothing seemed to effect Paul as he took every hit either by the arm, leg, or waist. When his patience finally thinned, he planted the heel of his boot once more onto the broken bone. It sounded like somebody snapped a stick.

That's when Bethany went out cold. Her arms dropped carelessly beside her when everything suddenly went dark. Paul still wasn't finished as he knelt over her unconscious body with his hands ready to tear open her garments. His fury with the broken rule would linger for a while and he'd take every single second on her hide. He broke apart Bethany's top, snapping all three buttons from the thread. Two of them danced along the floorboards. The other one flew clean across the kitchen and landed beside the ice box. Baring both her breasts, Paul attempted to finish destroying the dress until he heard Ava's voice.

"I know who you are," she said.

Paul wiped his sweaty hair from his face and saw Ava standing by the open door.

"You stay out of this wench," he shouted. "Go upstairs to your room."

"How could you've kept it a secret for this long?"

Paul left Bethany's exposed body behind as he stood up. The heart in his chest thumped an unpleasant migraine to the back of his eyes. Whatever he could see, darkened with the water splotches in his vision as his heart pumped faster.

"What are you talking about?" he said. Now, the tension started to tighten as he clenched both fists ready to make a deadly blow to the face.

"How'd it feel, Uncle?"

Shocked by what he heard, Paul stopped.

"How'd you find out?" he asked.

"I've found many things," she said. "I know about the boarding house. Do you want to know why Bethany knows? I told her. I've been crossing the boundary for quite some time now. And do you want to know the interesting part? You've been oblivious all this time."

Paul ground his teeth together as he chased Ava outside in the blistering cold. Snow flakes continued to fall around them as Paul pushed his wife into the mounds of snow. Clusters of it collapsed, making the effort to use any muscle power complicated. Paul searched for Ava by clawing at the snow like a bear. Ava used that moment to crawl her way towards the chapel where the graves lay silently. When Paul spotted Ava by the chapel door, he leaped over the mounds, and kicked her body in. The door snapped in half, sending the hinges and nails to the snow.

Ava gasped at the pain in her side as the pages nailed to the walls flapped in the wind. Paul had lit several candles earlier by the alter where her aching body had taken a tumble. She rocked her back against the alter, dropping the candles to the floor. The purple alter cloth caught the flame, causing an uproar of fire within the chapel. Paul didn't seem to mind as he stood by the opening with blood running from his teeth. His eyes had turned yellow from the flames behind Ava.

"What an adventure it has been," Paul said, stepping over loose shards of door. The walls began to melt around her as the pages took off. She watched it all burn around her as Paul came closer. Some of the roof caved in, making them flinch at the dust and debris. Ava saw the steel Cross lying amongst the debris a foot away. And for some odd reason, it was the only object amongst the pile of wood that didn't burn.

Paul knelt in front of Ava's hurting body with a grin stretched across his face. He looked like an evil troll that finally caught the girl crossing over his forbidden bridge.

"You will perish in this fire," he promised. "Bethany and I will continue our lives here at Lot. 4-06 and more wives will take your place. I can promise you that. This burning chapel isn't a bad idea really. I'm so glad you thought of it. Cannot end in a better way as I see it, niece. And don't worry about Bethany. Once I stay to watch you burn, I'll be sure to make that woman suffer as long as I can. Too bad you won't be here to see it."

The left wall suddenly collapsed, causing Paul to loose his balance. He fell to his left side when Ava reached over to retrieve the steel Cross. The steel began to melt the skin off her hand when she drove the sharp Cross into Paul's right hand. Blood splattered across the floorboards as if somebody had squashed a meaty caterpillar. Paul shouted in pain as he clenched the Cross with his other hand.

Ava managed to limp halfway across the chapel floor before she turned to look back. The fire grew massive as Paul tried to loosen the steel from his impaled hand. The object had melted clean to the bone and the wood, making it impossible to escape. Realizing death was close upon him, he turned to face Ava for the last time.

"I forgive you Paul," she said. "Only God knows I do."

Before Ava could hear his response , the burning chapel collapsed on top of Paul, burying him and everything beneath it.

28

The chapel burnt for a solid hour before dozens of police officers and firefighters responded to the billowing smoke cloud. Ava kept her place by the porch with a cover on her shoulders as several EMT employees worked on getting Bethany onto a portable stretcher. The agony Bethany had gone through tormented Ava as she watched from outside. But once she was on the stretcher and feeling somewhat comfortable, they began to move her out. Ava met Bethany by her side as the few remaining moments of the cabin and the burnt chapel slowly started to exit their lives forever.

"How are you feeling?" Ava said.

Ava had managed to motivate Bethany to smile a little.

"Broken," she answered. "But I'll be fine."

The team hoisted the stretcher over a tree stump in the same direction towards Ava's stream. The chapel had just got done being sprayed by several thick hoses. Four firefighters all dressed in their heavy gear watched Ava and the stretcher pass them by as the sizzled chapel issued its last breath of smoke into the atmosphere. The cabin seemed to disappear rapidly behind them until it looked like a little ant on a hill.

Ava felt something in her hand. She looked down and noticed it was Bethany's.

"Promise me we will always stay together," she said, coughing.

Ava topped Bethany's hand with hers and nodded.

"Sisters forever," Ava said. "I promise."

29

Ava and Bethany managed to adapt to a modern lifestyle in the small town of Chambers in Clearfield County, Pennsylvania. Although the transition seized to come easy, they figured anything was better than what they had gone through with Paul. Ava had gone onto college while Bethany maintained her employment at a local YMCA. The leg took several months to heal and the doctor warned there would be reasonable scarring to the tissue. Other than a small limp, Bethany was able to walk again.

Ava also introduced Christ to her life, feeling it was perhaps the most important aspect she had adjusted to her lifestyle. Bethany got Ava involved at the Church of Chambers with some help by the church administrator who went by the name of Margret Sheffield. It took Ava a while before she felt comfortable at the church. Living six years with a religious psychopath takes a toll on the spiritual mindset after a while but once things started happening, Ava soon realized she had missed something very important in her life.

A request was turned in to the town's sheriff to burn Lot. 4-06. The sheriff granted this request and once the state was onboard with the idea, the house was burned to the ground. Ava and Bethany received invites considering they played a major role there, but they turned it down for numerous, unspecified reasons.

Two bodies were recovered by the chapel site. Both of them had received proper burials in the Salem cemetery two blocks down from Ava and Bethany's church. Their names were known as Lillian and Shawn. Shawn had made his way to the newspapers not too long after his mysterious disappearance. Once his news of discovery made it to the public once again, Ava and Bethany were not questioned.

As for the boarding house, George would spend the next lifetime in state prison for molestation of minors, excessive accounts of kidnapping, and first-degree murder. The jury assigned to the case wasn't a pushover when it came to these types of charges. Police discovered fifteen young girls living in the boarding house. All of them were found to be related in some way and were ordered by the state to be boarded at a reasonable boarding house for adults in Chambers.

The chapel's remains were examined and investigated by the state police. Several items were bagged as evidence such as several pieces of unburnt Bible pages, nails, half of an alter, and a Cross buried into the charcoal floorboards. Paul's body was never accounted for.

30

Seven years later...

The sun felt warm on Ava's shoulders when Bethany sat down beside her with a glass of fresh squeezed lemonade. They siphoned the chunky contents through their straws as they watched from the grassy knoll as a small boy plummeted into the cold stream water from a knotted rope. Ava clapped and laughed when the boy rose to the surface in a toothless grin.

Bethany adjusted her candy cane bathing suit and reached for Ava's hand.

"Today would have been your anniversary," Bethany said. "Do you feel any different."

Ava finished her lemonade.

"Of course I feel different," she said. "I have nothing to worry about anymore."

"Do you still get your dreams?"

"Every night."

The boy climbed the wooden spokes along the tree trunk while holding onto the rope. He planted his heel on the knot, counted to three, and sailed into the breeze before letting go.

Splash!

"What do your dreams tell you this time?"

Ava thought about it for a moment while she watched the boy swim back to the rotten bank. He grabbed onto the roots and went straight for the tree again. The sunlight didn't touch down there like it did by the knoll. Cicadas were everywhere, rattling their behinds, signifying that fall was on its way.

"They give me a daunting feeling that Paul's not really dead," she said. "I feel like he's out there somewhere, watching."

"It bothers you that the state police never found his body, doesn't it?"

"Every day," Ava said. "I know he'll come searching for us one day, Beth. And when that day comes, he'll want something that belongs to him."

They both looked at the boy swinging across the stream on his rope. Bethany invested her trust in Ava's dreams, realizing that maybe their battle with Paul had only just begun. But it was seven years since the burning. How could he possibly know where they were?

"I got you a present today," Bethany said, turning to her side. She presented a bright blue box to the sunlight. Ava grinned as she opened the lid, revealing a small portable record player. Beside it was a Zombies record.

"What do you think?" Bethany asked smiling. "Your very own record player."

Ava reached across and hugged Bethany tightly.

"I love you," she whispered. "Always have and always will."

Bethany snickered before she lifted the record player out and snapped the Zombies record in snug. Clocking the needle in just right, *Time of the Season* began to play. The last time Bethany had heard it was seven years ago.

"Come on," Bethany said, grabbing Ava's hand. "Your son Liam is waiting for us."

Ava and Bethany ran towards Liam as he crawled out from the stream. He giggled as they chased him around in the shining sun. The record continued to play as the wind whistled between the oaks, joining their song with the cicadas. It was a beautiful day for the family.

And standing in the woods eighty yards from the stream bank stood a shadow amongst the darkness, waiting patiently for *its* turn to shine.

ABOUT THE AUTHOR

Cody Eichelberger lives with his wife Brittany Eichelberger in Chambersburg, Pennsylvania with their two dogs. If you wish to contact Cody Eichelberger, please feel free to send an email to the following email address: eichelbergercodyj4@gmail.com.

Book reservations, autographs, and future works can also be found on Facebook. The profile picture on Facebook is signified by the following picture for guidance: **CE**.

FIRST EDITION NOTICE

This novel is a true signed limited first edition, only if, the author signs the cover page, inscribes a designated number on the bottom of this page, and initials this page.

<u>34</u> of 200 (Limited Edition)

<u>CE</u>
CE

Made in the USA
Columbia, SC
30 August 2017